D0021489

SEARCHING FOR EMMA

SEARCHING FOR EMMA

Gustave Flaubert and
Madame Bovary

DACIA MARAINI

Translated by Vincent J. Bertolini

THE UNIVERSITY OF CHICAGO PRESS
Chicago & London

DACIA MARAINI has long been a leading figure in the Italian feminist movement. The author of numerous novels, poems, and plays, Maraini is also a prominent journalist. She won the Prix Formentor in 1963 with the publication of her second book, *The Age of Discontent*. Her books currently available in English translation are *Devour Me Too* (1987), *Letters to Marina* (1987), *The Train* (1989), *Woman at War* (1989), *The Silent Duchess* (1992), *Isolina* (1994), *Only Prostitutes Marry in May* (1995), *Bagheria* (1995), and *Voices* (1997).

VINCENT J. BERTOLINI is a lecturer in the Department of Romance Languages and Literatures at the University of Chicago.

The University of Chicago Press, Chicago 60637
The University of Chicago Press, Ltd., London

© 1998 by The University of Chicago
All rights reserved. Published 1998

Printed in the United States of America

07 06 05 04 03 02 01 00 99 98   1 2 3 4 5

ISBN: 0-226-50430-1 (cloth)

Cercando Emma: Gustave Flaubert e la Signora Bovary—indagini attorno a un romanzo, by Dacia Maraini, was originally published by Rizzoli. ©1993 RCS Rizzoli Libri S.p.A., Milano

Library of Congress Cataloging-in-Publication Data

Maraini, Dacia.
    [Cercando Emma. English]
    Searching for Emma : Gustave Flaubert and Madame Bovary / Dacia Maraini; translated by Vincent J. Bertolini.
        p.   cm.
    Includes bibliographical references and index.
    ISBN 0-226-50430-1 (cloth: alk. paper)
    1. Flaubert, Gustave, 1821–1880.   Madame Bovary.   2. Flaubert, Gustave, 1821–1880—Characters—Emma Bovary.   3. Characters and characteristics in literature.   I. Title.
PQ2246.M3M3713   1998
843′.8—dc21   97–23304
                                                                      CIP

♾ The paper used in this publication meets the minimum requirements of the American National Standard for Information Sciences—Permanence of Paper for Printed Library Materials, ANSI Z39.48–1984.

Translator's Note

Dacia Maraini's *Cercando Emma* is a lyrical, meditative, impressionistic account of Gustave Flaubert's several conflictual love relationships: that with his most famous female character, the beautiful, sentimental, desiring, and self-destructive Emma Bovary; that with his real-life lover of many years, the bohemian writer, activist, and proto-feminist Louise Colet; those with his literary brethren and cohorts Maxime Du Camp and Louis Bouilhet; and those with the many refractions of his own complex personality.

Maraini's rich portrait of this trailblazer of literary modernism draws on her reading of *Madame Bovary* and on an eclectic pastiche of other texts. Most often these are letters by, to, or about Flaubert. But Maraini's book is also built of quotations from literary works, biographies, and critical texts, most of which were originally composed in French, and none of which are cited in the kinds of formal academic footnotes so common in American critical essays.

Consequently, some of the labor of translating *Cercando Emma* involved approaching Maraini's abundant French sources through her Italian rendering of them. First, so as not to re-translate *Madame Bovary* from Maraini's Italian, I have employed Paul de Man's fine English translation for the many passages Maraini cites from Flaubert's novel. Similarly, where Maraini quotes from Flaubert's voluminous *Correspondance*, I have used published English versions of those passages, modifying them where it seemed important to preserve the flavor of Maraini's own translation. Where no English version of a particular passage from a letter or other text was found or where the published English version seemed inadequate, I was constrained to translate that passage through the Italian. The problem of accuracy was then resolved through the painstaking process of checking my English back against the original French. I am grateful to Margaret Mahan and her assistant, Jenni Fry, at the University of Chicago Press for their help in safeguarding my translation from the inaccuracies such leaps between languages might have caused.

For Maraini's quotations from the journals of the Goncourt brothers and from Louise Colet's literary works, I have turned to published versions both in French and in English, citing them in standard footnote form. In these and in all other cases, the numbered footnotes in this edition are my own and did not appear in the original Italian edition of *Cercando Emma*. I have, however, tried to keep them to a minimum, to preserve the essayistic character of Maraini's book.

In a handful of cases, where original French versions of quoted passages could not be located—there appear to be no editions, for instance, of the collected correspondence of either Louis Bouilhet or Maxime Du Camp in any American library—I have confidently relied on the accuracy of Maraini's Italian rendering.

Notwithstanding the several technical complications involved in translating *Cercando Emma*, Maraini's book provided me with many pleasurable hours of struggle, as I endeavored to capture in English the subtlety of her tone, the aptness of her tropes, or the fluidity of her style, which interweaves the elegant and belletristic with the contemporary and colloquial. I hope I have been able to faithfully represent both the creative and the critical dimensions of a nimble Italian mind as it puts Flaubert's psychobiography into conversation with his masterpiece, one of the most famous European novels ever published. What emerges from this colloquy is an intriguing picture of the intellect and personality of a major figure in nineteenth-century French literary culture. But *Cercando Emma* is also valuable because it allows us to glimpse, through Maraini's perceptive reading of the letters between Flaubert, Louise Colet, and others, a suggestive world of relationships between friends, lovers, and fellow artists during a period of transition in the history of Western gender relations and romantic and erotic mores.

Vincent J. Bertolini
University of Chicago

French Texts Consulted

Bellet, Roger. *Femmes de lettres au XIXe siècle: Autour de Louise Colet.* Lyon: University of Lyon Press, 1982.
Bood, Micheline, and Serge Grand. *L'Indomptable Louise Colet.* Paris: Pierre Horay, 1986.

Colet, Louise. *Ce qu'on rêve en aimant: Poésies nouvelles.* Paris: Librairie Nouvelle, 1854.

Flaubert, Gustave. *Les Oeuvres de Gustave Flaubert.* Edited by Maurice Nadeau. 18 vols. Lausanne: Société Coopérative Editions Recontre, 1964.

———. *Oeuvres complètes de Gustave Flaubert.* 9 vols. Paris: Louis Conard, 1926.

———. *Voyages.* Edited by René Dumesnil. 2 vols. Paris: Société les Belles Lettres, 1948.

Goncourt, Edmond and Jules de. *Journal: Mémoires de la vie littéraire.* 20 vols. Monaco: Fasquelle and Flammarion, 1956.

English Texts Consulted

Barnes, Julian. *Flaubert's Parrot.* New York: Alfred A. Knopf, 1985.

Colet, Louise. *"Lui": A View of Him.* Translated by Marilyn Gaddis Rose. Athens, Ga.: University of Georgia Press.

du Plessix Gray, Francine. *Rage and Fire: A Life of Louise Colet, Pioneer Feminist, Literary Star, Flaubert's Muse.* New York: Simon & Schuster, 1994.

Flaubert, Gustave. *Madame Bovary.* Edited and translated by Paul de Man. New York: W. W. Norton & Co.

———. *Letters of Gustave Flaubert.* Edited by Richard Rumbold. Translated by J. M. Cohen. London: George Weidenfeld & Nicholson Limited, 1950.

———. *The Selected Letters of Gustave Flaubert.* Edited and translated by Francis Steegmuller. New York: Farrar, Straus and Young, 1953.

———. *The Letters of Gustave Flaubert, 1830–1857.* Edited and translated by Francis Steegmuller. Cambridge, Mass.: Harvard University Press, 1980.

———. *The Letters of Gustave Flaubert, 1857–1880.* Edited and translated by Francis Steegmuller. Cambridge, Mass.: Harvard University Press, 1982.

Goncourt, Edmond and Jules de. *The Goncourt Journals, 1851–1870.* Edited and translated by Lewis Galantière. Garden City, N.Y.: Doubleday, Doran & Co., 1937.

⋙ SEARCHING FOR EMMA ⋘

Emma Bovary is one of those old family friends in the neighborhood of our minds. We seem to have known her forever; her entire history is familiar to us.

For years we've heard it said that Emma is Flaubert's most beloved creation, so much so that he was moved to identify with her publicly: "*Madame Bovary,*" he wrote, "*c'est moi.*" We've heard that Emma's infidelity is revealed, scrutinized, and pursued by her author with deep empathy, almost as if the novel argued for the freedom of female love within the narrow confines of the bourgeois marriage, in a society permeated by the banal and the commonplace.

And yet in my memory of the first time I read the novel—with adolescent enthusiasm (I was sixteen)—I recall a lingering feeling of unease, almost of distress, though not due to the risqué nature of the theme, nor even to Emma's horrible final punishment, which took my breath away. My distress arose instead from the mocking, angry way the author had introduced me to this woman.

I did not understand at the time that this was a matter of viewpoint. As a young female reader, I had immersed myself in the beautiful dark waters of the novel and had lost my powers of discrimination. I had no idea from which directions the blows were coming. And the blows came hard on someone like me, a reader who desperately wanted to understand and sympathize with the protagonist.

Emma seemed to be a tragic figure, the victim of a suffocating marriage, held hostage by a despicable and unworthy husband.

Today, as I revisit the novel, Emma still seems to be a hostage—but not so much to her husband as to her author, who pursues her with a ruthlessness and tenacity that verge on the grotesque, and with a bitter, mocking determination.

In the essay "Gustave Flaubert" (*Notes on Novelists*, 1914), Henry James writes, "Our complaint is that Emma Bovary, in spite of the nature of her consciousness and in spite of her reflecting so much that of her creator, is really too small an affair." And he asks himself, with anguish: "Why did Flaubert choose, as special conduits of the life he proposed to depict, such inferior . . . human specimens?"

I asked myself the same question on my first reading of the

1

novel, and I still ask it today. It is the reason I felt the need to write these pages, hoping to understand something more of this conundrum. I wanted to understand not only more about the relationship between Flaubert and Emma but more about the relationship between authors and their characters in general.

Given that female readers are more numerous than male readers, given that female readers love to identify themselves with female characters from novels, they sometimes contrive to find in the heroines of books qualities that these characters do not in fact have.

The tenacity of women readers is boundless, as boundless as their creative enthusiasm. They delve into books like knowing moles and try to shape literary characters after their own model, according to their deepest needs, careless of whether the traits attributed to a character of their desires truly correspond or not.

And so it happened that Emma Bovary, queen of a novel extraordinary for its visionary qualities and realistic details, was adopted by women readers as a standard-bearer, a pathfinder who, confronted with the sordidness of bourgeois marriage, sees the liberties she takes as "sacrosanct."

Few of these readers take time to look more closely at Emma, and at how her author judges her, moment by moment, drawing her character in minute detail. Women readers are given to adapt what they read in any way, so much so that they will take complete possession of that rarest of literary commodities: a strong female character with a visible will to action.

On first reading the novel, I, too, a voracious and naive female reader, saw in Madame Bovary the kind of brave and passionate woman I would like to have accompany me on my mental rambles, as you might like to be accompanied by a woman of strong mind, of firm but graceful tread.

It was years later, rereading Flaubert's beautiful and sensual novel, that I realized how detested Emma Bovary truly was, how many indignities her author had heaped upon her—so many that she is left without a single good quality, not one.

The novel begins radiantly with the scene, which everyone remembers, of a new student arriving at a country school. His name is Charles Bovary, a name he cannot even clearly pronounce, garbling it as "Charbovari." He is clumsy, awkward, embarrassed, and moves heavily. At his mere appearance his classmates break into laughter. The teacher makes the poor boy write twenty times, on a sheet from his notebook, *ridiculus sum*.

And yet, in this same beginning there is something that leaves us unsettled, doubtful. This confusion arises when we realize that a first-person narrative voice, a flesh-and-blood "I" initially present, has mysteriously disappeared without our ever finding out why.

It seems strange that an author as precise as Flaubert would not have accounted for this. Strange, that is, unless this oversight represents some hidden sign pointing to a secret door in the novel for us to open.

The first chapter begins, "We were in class when the headmaster came in," a sentence which implies the choice of a specific point of view: a witness, a personal memory, someone who will tell us about a schoolmate who later became a doctor in Yonville, and so on.

But this narrator vanishes by the end of the first chapter. Is this a deliberate loss, a whim, forgetfulness, some kind of slip?

Given the almost insane meticulousness of the writer, I would say that this disappearing narrator suggests instead a kind of cue placed at the beginning of the novel which indicates the ambiguous point of view that will accompany the whole book. So as to truly confuse the reader, Flaubert patches the entire novel out of uncertainties of narrative perspective, which in turn constitute its subtle originality.

This is the only way to understand Flaubert's declaration "I am Madame Bovary." His writing in this novel works like a false mirror that, while reflecting the image of a beautiful young woman with black hair parted into two smooth folds, also hints that behind the surface stands a more robust and virile body, one which enjoys dissimulating itself through the delicate features of a restless and impulsive woman. Flaubert could not help but imagine being "the other," as Sartre remarked in *The Family Idiot*, and he also loved to play the man of action, simply because the role satisfied him.

Flaubert's book can certainly be read in various ways: as a pitiless portrait, analytic and realistic, of a provincial French adultress
of the nineteenth century; as a lampoon of a certain cultural myth;
as a critique of a flighty, impulsive personality; as an anatomy of
everyday language; as a highly wrought and naturalistic portrait of
a provincial countrywoman and her shabby, ridiculous compeers;
even as a novel about the bitter humor of nothingness. "What
seems beautiful to me, what I should like to write, is a book about
nothing," Flaubert wrote to Louise Colet on January 16, 1852.

The various readings the text encompasses are all valid in their
way. Yet this text continually reveals vague signs of unease, which
render it a perfectly ambiguous, and perfectly wonderful, book.

I will try here to gather up the pebbles dropped by Emma on
the paths of the forest, to see if they carry us toward the house of
impossible desire or toward something more obscure and unforeseen.

The first time we meet her, Emma is still a young, untutored girl living in her father's house on a farm in the country.

When Charles Bovary sets eyes upon her, Emma is standing at the front door with a polite smile upon her lips, wearing a "blue merino dress with three flounces."

Blue, sky blue, royal blue often accompany the descriptions of Emma's beauty. Though her eyes are black, as Flaubert almost regretfully specifies, something celestial, like a halo of spirituality, always encircles her. We will soon learn, however, that in Emma there is absolutely nothing heavenly to be found. The blue is there only to reveal something about her ambiguous graces, her dazzling sensuality.

The young doctor Charles Bovary has just graduated from medical school, not without difficulty, since his laziness induced him to drag out his studies for years. It is his mother, finally, who forces him to finish his degree; she then finds him both a medical position in Tostes and an elderly wife with a good dowry—the widow Madame Dubuc of the bony arms, the icy feet, and the skin with "as many pimples as the spring has buds."

The doctor is hauled from his bed that fateful morning by a letter stamped with blue sealing wax (a glimpse of the color that will envelop his senses for the rest of his life?) which calls him to the Bertaux farm to set the broken leg of Monsieur Rouault, Emma's father.

"The fracture was a simple one, without any kind of complication," Flaubert explains, immediately casting doubt upon the medical capacities of the young Bovary. But, caught up in the fervor of inexperience, the novice immediately begins giving orders for bandages and splints to bind up the leg of *père* Rouault. The maid is sent in search of wood in the barn; Emma is asked to sew some small cushions to be inserted between the skin and the splint.

Though the young Emma has yet to be physically described to us—save for that brief mention of the blue dress of merino wool—Flaubert gives us a hint of her character. Her father, seeing her dawdle as she looks for her needle case, loses his patience and, annoyed, scolds her. However unfair the rebuke, Emma says nothing. Instead, she begins to sew rapidly and, in her haste, pricks her fingers, which she then "put to her mouth to suck them."

Just as the evil fairy predicts that Sleeping Beauty will prick herself and fall into a fatal sleep—from which she will be able to reawaken, the good fairy adds to the prediction, only when a prince in blue kisses her—so we can imagine Emma, with that pinprick, falling into the long sleep of marriage, from which she will be awakened only by the kiss of adultery.

The author intends at the beginning of the story to introduce us to an Emma submissive and suffused in blue. But we will soon learn that her submissiveness and her filial devotion are only theatrical techniques, since Emma, as we will come to find out, loves to act. She knows nothing of either sincerity or the critical spirit. And she loves, too, to keep changing roles; otherwise, she gets bored.

The first part that Emma plays for her readers is that of the marriageable girl, bashful, obedient, and chaste, daughter of a gruff but good-natured father. At this point in the story, perhaps, she doesn't know she is acting. She still does it instinctively, just as she instinctively modulates her voice so that "according to what she was saying, her voice was clear, sharp, or, suddenly all languor, lingering out in modulations that ended almost in murmurs as she spoke to herself."

In addition to the blue of her dress, the other thing which attracts Charles's gaze is the whiteness of Emma's nails: "They were shiny, delicate at the tips, more polished than the ivory of Dieppe, and almond-shaped."

And yet, as the author tells us, her hand could not exactly be called beautiful, since it was "perhaps not white enough, and a little hard at the knuckles; besides, it was too long, with no soft inflections in the outlines."

Her eyes, however, are judged unqualifiedly beautiful: "Although brown, they seemed black because of the lashes." And those beautiful eyes were turned upon the unknown doctor with a "candid boldness."

The gaze Charles returns to her is alert, and not devoid of critical spirit—a spirit which, over the course of their marriage, will gradually wane until it vanishes.

Monsieur Rouault invites the doctor to "have a bite" with them before he heads back to Tostes. So the three go downstairs to the dining room on the ground floor. "There was an odor of iris-root and damp sheets" in the room piled with sacks of wheat. And one curious detail: a charcoal drawing of the head of Minerva, under which appeared in Gothic letters the phrase "To my dear Papa."

Two facts, therefore, are called to our attention that contradict our first impression of Mademoiselle Emma Rouault's submissiveness and self-control: the eyes, which gaze with "candid boldness," and the head of Minerva, which, although humbly dedicated to her father, hints at something quite different from surrender, perhaps even some bellicose intent: Minerva is an armed goddess.

We are subsequently informed that "Mademoiselle Rouault did not at all like the country" where her father resided, and even less now that, since her mother's death, "she had to look after the farm almost alone."

Her father does not, in turn, find her assistance indispensable but, rather, feels that his daughter is "too clever for farming, a calling under the ban of Heaven, since one never saw a millionaire in it."

He and Charles Bovary both see the girl as a flower too delicate (that alabaster skin, those tender hands, those tiny Parisian feet, those beautifully adorned blue dresses) to be left to languish on a farm, among cows and sheep.

"Her neck stood out from a white turned-down collar. Her hair, whose two black folds seemed each of a single piece, so smooth were they, was parted in the middle by a delicate line that curved slightly with the curve of the head; and, just showing the tip of the ear, it was joined behind in a thick chignon, with a wavy movement at the temples that the country doctor saw now for the first time in his life. The upper part of her cheek was rose-coloured. Like a man, she wore a tortoise-shell eyeglass thrust between two buttons of her blouse."

Here another detail contradicts her initial appearance. What are those men's glasses doing on Emma Rouault's very feminine dress (of blue merino with three flounces)? Are they not there to tell us that Emma is hiding, or only partially revealing, something about herself that makes her different from the way she would like to appear? Something that, in the eye of the acute observer, seems meaningful only in the context of all the fleeting hints of a contradictory personality?

Your image will stay with me all imbued with poetry and tenderness, as last night was bathed in the milky vapor of its silvery mist.

(August 8, 1846)

Ah! Our two carriage rides in the Bois; how beautiful they were, particularly the second, with the lightning flashes above us. I find myself remembering the color of the trees lit by the streetlights, and the swaying motion of the springs. We were alone, happy: I kept staring at you, and even in the darkness your whole face seemed illumined by your eyes.

(August 4, 1846)

These are passages from letters that Gustave Flaubert wrote to Louise Colet shortly after meeting her, during one of his rare sojourns in Paris, at the house of the sculptor James Pradier, and five years before sitting down to write *Madame Bovary*.

Why do I cite them? Because reading the correspondence of Flaubert—a miser in his novelistic production, but a prodigious letter writer, who dashed off letters in a fluid and expansive style that sparkled with wit and irony—I could not help but recognize Emma in Louise and Louise in Emma.

Madame Bovary, as his friends said time and again—they even proposed its subject to Flaubert after pronouncing his *Temptation of Saint Anthony* a failure—was based on the Delamare case, a famous incident made much of by the popular press of the period.

Delphine Couturier Delamare, a woman overwhelmed by debt, had killed herself; afterward, her husband discovered from her hidden letters that she had taken lovers. The husband, Eugène Delamare, was a public health official.

This episode may well have been the basis for Flaubert's novel. But when it came to fleshing out the principal character, drawing Emma's personality, we cannot help but think that Flaubert naturally modeled her on someone whom he knew more intimately.

Furthermore, though it bears the traces of the emotions that characterized the story of the original "passion"—first impetuous, then violent and tragic—the novel gets thornier, grows increasingly skittish and artificial; the illicit encounters taper off and become more sporadic, through growing disaffection and, ultimately, hatred.

We discover Emma perfectly drawn in Gustave's letters to

Louise, recognizable in all her explosive contradictions: on the one hand, very feminine in her sweet and delicate enticements, in her tenderness and generosity, in her morbid and self-effacing attachment to her beloved; on the other, a bit masculine in her most brazen self-assertions, in her obsession with independence, in her combative spirit, in her bold-faced aggressiveness.

At the same time, we find in Emma traits of Louise that, though hidden or denied, also belong to Emma's creator: a certain adolescent hunger for the exotic, an infantile tendency toward fetishism, an ability to lose oneself in dreams, a theatrical boastfulness, an indolent sensuality, a love for the escapist white lie, a taste for the kinds of knickknacks that can at times pervert an artistic sensibility.

We may understand Emma better by knowing Louise and understand Flaubert better by knowing his letters, so extraordinary in their vitality, depth, exuberance, and sincerity.

The epistolary world of Flaubert is, however, populated for the most part by male figures, former schoolmates with whom he continued to correspond throughout his life. One of these, Ernest Chevalier, remained a close friend until his marriage, which Flaubert regarded as "a subtle betrayal." As boys they had a medallion inscribed with the words "Gustave and Ernest will never leave each other." Some of the letters to Ernest begin with the tender invocation "Return, life of my life, soul of my soul." They say things like "If by any chance you didn't come I'd go to Les Andelys to get you on all fours like the dogs of King Louis *Fils-Lippe*" (April 3, 1832?). They sometimes end "Your dauntless . . . friend till death" (February 4, 1831).

And then there was Alfred Le Poittevin, a classmate from boarding school, older by a year or so, whom his comrades called "a late–imperial Greek." "He was a sophist, affected the byzantine," Maxime Du Camp later said of him. "He loved metaphysical discussions. . . . He had a positive literary influence on Gustave. . . . He taught him the art of discipline in writing. . . . Together they dedicated themselves to literature, and they hid it like a crime."

This same Maxime Du Camp was to remain true to Flaubert to the end, through thick and thin, through moments of intense intimacy and endless quarrels, through backbiting, resolves to end the friendship, and sudden rapprochements.

9

But the most beloved of these early companions was without a doubt Louis Bouilhet. (In a strange twist of verbal fate, the wife of the sculptor Pradier, another woman whom Flaubert loved during a lapse of interest in Louise Colet, was also named Louise.)

Bouilhet, whom Gustave familiarly calls "my left ball," later became a writer, a dramatist, and, most important, an intelligent editor for Flaubert: he helped Flaubert untangle the intricacies of his most demanding literary project, *Madame Bovary*.

In addition, Gustave exchanged letters and visits with Ernest Feydeau, Jules Duplan, Guy de Maupassant, the Goncourt brothers, and Théophile Gautier.

The tone of the letters was often sophomoric, even infantile. "1st prize for solitary masturbation: Ronchin," we read in Flaubert's letter to Alfred Le Poittevin in the far-off years of 1837 and 1838. "1st prize (after me) for the duration of sodomitic desire, Morel. 1st prize for coming in one's underwear: Morel. 1st prize for *la côtelette:* Fargeau. 1st prize for the idiot stare: Fargeau. 1st prize for the excessively immoral stare, grand prize: Morel."

Then, in his twenty-ninth year, from Girgeh in Tunisia: "In Keneh I screwed a good-looking girl that loved me a lot and was giving me signals that I had beautiful eyes. Her name is Osneh-Taouileh, which means 'the long mare.' She's just another dirty slut that I enjoyed myself with and who curdled the butter. . . . Old man, try not to break your balls. Don't screw too much. Save your energy, an ounce of wasted sperm is worth more than ten pounds of blood" (June 2, 1850).

And then again, at age thirty-seven, from Croisset: "My ardent brother . . . you send me news of the arts, in return I will send you some news from the country: the bread baker of Croisset employs as an assistant a fat boy. Now the master baker and his helper f-ck . . . knead each other by the heat of the oven. But (and this is the good part) the above-mentioned baker possesses a wife, and these two gentlemen, not content to simply f-ck, roundly screw the poor creature. Together they bang away at her for fun, and for their mutual hatred of cunts (by the Jérôme method [named for a character in Sade's *Justine*]), with so much gusto that the poor woman cannot get out of bed for days thereafter" (August 28, 1858).

10

And Bouilhet is no less colorful: "Everything goes according to plan, Monsignor, we have the caviar and do enjoy it. . . . Do not forget to shake the hand of Abbot Duplan, dearest Vicar General" (March 14, 1862). These were their nicknames for each other, Grand Vicar and Monsignor. "Did you screw Lady Legier, Grand Vicar?" "To Monsieur Flahuberg, Hail, O Fiery Pen! Punic Paper-eater! Guzzler of books! Dreamer! Thundering Gorge! Peerless! Parisian! Voyager! Outlaw! Vagina-Sniffer! Garçon! I salute you, O you who are returning Saturday! sincerely yours, with heartfelt regards" (November 29, 1860). In another letter, he dedicates a poem on shit to Flaubert: "I love shit! a thing immortal! / perhaps one shouldn't, so I say it *sotto voce* / I am crazy for it. / . . . its great distinction is it comes from our ass, / that it's limpid and gorgeous / and people can sniff it and do not eat it" (October 2, 1857).

Flaubert never gives up this language—alternately scatological, sophomoric, swaggering, and provincial—not even when he is near death. On the contrary, writing and speaking like this was a way of staying young, of keeping adolescence alive through the tenderness, obscenity, and ribaldry of words.

These friends frequented bordellos and wrote texts together (Gustave Flaubert wrote *Par les champs et par les grèves* with Maxime Du Camp in 1847, after a long trip to Normandy and Brittany); together they debated, ate, slept, drank, dreamed. When one fell in love, he suffered the reproaches, but enjoyed the complicity, of the others. They constantly banded together, acting by turns as each other's mediators, advisors, proofreaders, censors, panders, always striving to keep intact the tiny, isolated world that they considered superior to every other.

It is three o'clock. The other inhabitants of the house are in the fields. "Some flies on the table were crawling up the glasses that had been used, and buzzing as they drowned themselves in the dregs of the cider."

Emma, charming in a summer dress which leaves her shoulders bare, offers Dr. Charles Bovary a glass of liqueur. He demurs, laughing. She insists. "He could see small drops of perspiration on her bare shoulders."

Emma, following provincial custom, pulls from the cabinet a bottle of curaçao. She pours it into two small glasses that she has placed on the table. One she hands to the handsome young doctor, and the other she carries to her lips. She finishes it off in one gulp, country-style. Timid, awkward, uncertain, he finally gives in and drinks his too.

Rather than putting her now empty glass down, Emma holds it upended on her tongue, to retrieve the last drops. Then, with the tip of her tongue, she "licked drop by drop" the last of the sugary liqueur sticking to the bottom of the glass.

This little seduction scene, as we can see, is represented almost filmically, with a wealth of visual details. It is a scene from which we deduce that Emma is capable of duplicity: on the one hand, she acts out the role of the good daughter, humble and obedient; on the other, she plays the game of the expert seductress according to her theatrical whim of the moment, in exactly the same way that she modulates her voice according to her moods and the circumstances.

Charles, however, is made of more uniform, stolid stuff. It is not that Emma doesn't interest him but, more probably, that adultery doesn't suit him, in the same way that he can't manage to lie because he lacks the imagination for it.

But things fall into place for Charles without his even lifting a hand, almost as if the gods keep watch over him and smooth the way before him. Not without suffering life's occasional cruelty, however.

A notary who makes off with all of his clients' money blows the lid off the financial situation of the widow Dubuc: "The house at Dieppe was found to be eaten up with mortgages to its foundations; what she had placed with the notary God only knew. . . .

12

She had lied, the good lady! In his exasperation, Monsieur Bovary the elder, smashing a chair on the stone floor, accused his wife of having caused the misfortune of their son by harnessing him to such a harridan, whose harness wasn't worth her hide."

Father and mother Bovary rush to Tostes to discuss the matter with their son. "There were scenes. Héloise in tears, throwing her arms about her husband, conjured him to defend her from his parents. Charles tried to speak up for her. They grew angry and left the house."

It is a vulgar but familiar scene and causes the worst sorts of emotions to burst forth—all, of course, in the name of protecting the interests of their beloved son. They had wanted him to get married, against his will, to a rich widow well past her prime, but when she finds herself broke, they hurl themselves upon her, cursing her and calling her "harridan." Charles proves himself to be far more tactful and humane than his parents. He doesn't rage against his wife, Héloise, but takes her side instead. He defends her even though he knows that it will irritate and offend his parents. He is tenderhearted and compassionate.

But now, as Flaubert cynically writes, "'The blow had struck home.' A week after, as she was hanging up some washing in her yard, she was seized with a spitting of blood, and the next day, while Charles had his back turned and was closing the window curtains, she said, 'O God!' gave a sigh and fainted. She was dead! What a surprise!"

Now Charles is free to hurry to the side of his beloved Emma, but he does not do it. He reacts in a way consistent with his character, which is lazy, slow, meditative. "When all was over at the cemetery Charles went home. He found no one downstairs; he went up to the first floor to their room, saw her dress still hanging at the foot of the alcove; then leaning against the writing-table, he stayed until the evening, buried in a sorrowful reverie. She had loved him after all!"

Several days later, Charles receives a visit from old Rouault, who conveys his condolences and invites Charles to call at the farm again. He accepts, though without that invitation he would probably have allowed much more time to pass before making a decision. Perhaps he would have given up any idea of marrying again.

Right up to the very end, Charles's character will never betray itself, made up as it is of laziness, gentleness of spirit, naïveté, clumsiness, and immaturity. Are these not facets of the native but repressed character of Flaubert?

Let us not forget, however, that Emma is the protagonist of this novel. After the brief, cruel digression on the death of the widow Dubuc, the story returns to Emma and to her past, recounted to the reader with ironic maliciousness.

Emma's childhood, we are told, was a perfectly predictable one: "Brought up at the Ursuline convent," she "had received what is called 'a good education', and so knew dancing, geography, drawing, how to embroider and play the piano." Moreover, she read constantly.

In the convent, she proved pious and diligently performed her duties—so diligently, in fact, that the sisters spoke of a "profound vocation," which would most surely lead to her taking the veil. As a result, they surrounded her with the most minute cares and attentions.

But Emma was by no means interested in the relationship between the soul and God, Flaubert tells us. "Living . . . without ever leaving the warm atmosphere of the class-rooms, and amid these pale-faced women wearing rosaries with brass crosses, she was softly lulled by the mystic languor exhaled in the perfumes of the altar, the freshness of the holy water, and the lights of the tapers," rather than by any true religious feeling.

Hers was a completely aesthetic and sensual rapport with the rituals of the church, born of emotional longing or literary fantasy. In fact, "instead of following mass, she looked at the pious vignettes with their azure borders in her book, and she loved the sick lamb, the sacred heart pierced with sharp arrows, or the poor Jesus sinking beneath the cross he carried." Flaubert suggests that her religious feeling is infantile, that it travesties the sacred.

When she went to confession, she even "invented little sins in order that she might stay there longer, kneeling in the shadow, her hands joined, her face against the grating beneath the whispering of the priest."

She liked to think of Christ as "betrothed, husband, celestial lover," and these thoughts evoked within her soul "depths of unexpected sweetness."

Her every moment of contemplation had to have some kind of utility: "She had to gain some personal profit from things and she rejected as useless whatever did not contribute to the immediate satisfaction of her heart's desires—being of a temperament more sentimental than artistic, looking for emotions, not landscapes."

She read romance novels that a friend lent her surreptitiously which spoke of faraway lovers, faithful and dreaming, of "heartaches, vows, sobs, tears and kisses, little boatrides by moonlight, nightingales in shady groves, gentlemen brave as lions, gentle as lambs, virtuous as no one ever was, always well dressed, and weeping like fountains."

At fifteen, Emma had already read many books. "For six months . . . Emma dirtied her hands with the greasy dust of old lending libraries. With Walter Scott, . . . she fell in love with historical events, dreamed of guardrooms, old oak chests, and minstrels. She would have liked to live in some old manor-house, like those long-waisted chatelaines who, in the shade of pointed arches, spent their days leaning on the stone, chin in hand, watching a white-plumed knight galloping on his black horse from the distant fields."

Not many authors are so precise and punctilious in the way they describe the literary tastes of their characters. Have no doubt, Flaubert seems to tell us, that from adolescence on Emma went in for some of the worst literature of the period. She became possessed by it; it intoxicated her.

It is the insistence with which Flaubert vilifies Emma's literary tastes that amazes us, as if those were the true sins to condemn, and everything else merely the consequence of such reading.

Emma loved "illustrious or unhappy women. Joan of Arc, Héloise, Agnès Sorel, the beautiful Ferronière, and Clémence Isaure stood out to her like comets in the dark immensity of history." The girls who boarded at convents at that time used to hide under their pillows satin-bound books of verse signed by viscounts and viscountesses. "Emma trembled as she blew back the thin transparent paper over the engraving and saw it folded in two and fall gently against the page. Here behind the balustrade of a balcony was a young man in a short cloak, holding in his arms a young girl in a white dress who was wearing an alms-bag at her belt; or there were nameless portraits of English ladies with fair curls, who looked at you from under their round straw hats with their large clear eyes."

The heroines of such books always have "a tear on their cheeks." Or they are intent upon "kissing doves through the bars of a Gothic cage." Or better, "smiling, their heads on one side, . . . plucking the leaves of a marguerite with their taper fingers." Not to mention the sultans, "reclining beneath arbours in the arms of Bayadères; . . . Tartar minarets on the horizon, Roman ruins in the foreground with some kneeling camels."

And what of music? "The ballads [Emma] sang were all about little angels with golden wings, madonnas, lagunes, gondoliers; harmless-sounding compositions that, in spite of the inanity of the style and the vagueness of the melody, enabled one to catch a glimpse of the tantalizing phantasmagoria of sentimental realities." Emma delights in everything that today we call kitsch, cultural refuse, the half-chewed remains of old aristocratic myths, the wreckage of cheap philosophies, oriental borrowings.

The doggedness with which Flaubert rages against such cultural waste is cruel, calculated, at times even methodical. His lists follow each other page after page, and they remind us of a book he wrote years later and left unfinished, *Bouvard and Pécuchet*, in which he strove to compile in one volume all of the enormous nonsense, fabulous stupidities, and tumultuous aspirations to culture of two good-for-nothings in love with books.

W hen her mother died, Emma "cried much," Flaubert re- lates. But, immediately thereafter, he adds "the first few days": the poignance of her pain will soon become dulled by her taste for theater. "She had a funeral picture made with the hair of the deceased, and, in a letter sent to the Bertaux full of sad reflec- tions on life, she asked to be buried later on in the same grave."

Rouault, alarmed, sets out immediately to find out whether by chance his daughter has fallen prey to some nervous affliction, what today we might call a depression. But Emma is just fine. And when she sees her father returning, she is extremely happy, since her performance has turned out a success: "She had reached at a first attempt the rare ideal of delicate lives, never attained by mediocre hearts." With renewed vigor, "she let herself meander along with Lamartine, listened to harps on lakes, to all the songs of dying swans, to the falling of the leaves, the pure virgins ascend- ing to heaven, and the voice of the Eternal discoursing down the valleys."

Lamartine is an object of Flaubert's particular antipathy: he considered him flowery, affected, and sentimental, a young ladies' writer, to be exact. "The last word in pretentious stupidity," he writes of *Raphaël* in a letter to Louise Colet (May 2, 1852).

"The number of ready-made hemistiches, of verses that are empty paraphrases, is incredible," he writes a year later of another of Lamartine's books, *Jocelyn*. "When he attempts to paint the more vulgar aspects of life, he just can't get it right. . . . His poetry is detestable, inane, doesn't breathe. Those sentences have no muscle, no blood. What a peculiar vision of human existence!" (May 17, 1853).

Flaubert had to swallow all of these harsh judgments when, at the censorship trial of *Madame Bovary*, Lamartine generously and publicly took the part of the accused writer. "I am considerably surprised," Gustave writes to his brother Achille on January 18, 1857, "I should never have expected the creator of Elvire to fall in love with Homais!"

Emma's performances have the advantage of lasting only a short time. Indeed, she herself is the first to become bored by them. After a while even dying swans and fallen leaves make her nauseous. But, as often happens to those who make a practice of performing, she doesn't find it easy to quit without losing some credibility. Therefore she persists in her fiction, says Flaubert, but without any real commitment to the game: she "continued from habit first, then out of vanity. . . . The good nuns, who had been so sure of her vocation, perceived with great astonishment that Mademoiselle Rouault seemed to be slipping from them."

Emma's only desire now is to return home so she can dedicate herself to "ruling over the servants." But, naturally, she will also pursue this "rule" to the point of utter boredom and will wind up "miss[ing] her convent."

Emma's feelings are exactly the ones we find described in Flaubert's letters: "It's pitiful, but I've always been this way, continuously craving what I don't have, and not knowing how to enjoy it when I do have it, and so I get distressed and frighten myself about the evils which will befall me. . . . If I were to lose you I might go crazy. So it goes in the coherent incoherence of the human heart, in the nature of man. And I am truly a man, in the most vulgar and truest sense of the word, even if in the blindness of your love you believe me to be a more elevated being" (December 7, 1846).

When Charles appears at the Bertaux farm, Emma already considers herself "quite disillusioned, with nothing more to learn, and nothing more to feel."

She is a "corrupt" girl, as Flaubert says, who no longer distinguishes between real feelings and feelings coldly acted out, between feverish fantasies of characters from books and real people.

Her only pleasure is feeling that fleeting thrill that one gets from seeing one's life represented on stage. Such a thing, Flaubert suggests, is not bad in and of itself but becomes bad when this mise-en-scène is crude and in poor taste.

Old Rouault has said yes to Charles Bovary's request for Emma's hand in marriage. As for Emma, she already dreams of another grand theatricalization. In order to escape the house of her father, to make herself the protagonist (now adult) of a new story, to free herself from the exhausting responsibilities of life on the farm, Emma will go to the lengths of imagining herself to be in love with Charles.

"The uneasiness of her new position, or perhaps the disturbance caused by the presence of this man, had sufficed to make her believe that she at last felt that wondrous passion which, till then, like a great bird with rose-coloured wings, hung in the splendor of poetic skies."

Emma dreams of a magnificent marriage ceremony with torches and dances in the darkness. Fortunately, her father prohibits it. She must be content with a big dinner party and forty-three guests. Her dress is ostentatious, and the meal winds up lasting sixteen hours.

Flaubert's eye nastily observes the marriage ceremony: "It was [Charles] who might . . . have been taken for the virgin of the evening before, whilst the bride gave no sign that revealed anything." She was only mildly exuberant, the way an expert actress on the most prestigious of stages would be.

Conjugal life begins to take on its own rhythm, composed of tedious little rituals that begin to bore the young bride after only a few months. Every morning Charles leaves the house very early on the back of his old mare, blowing a kiss to his wife from the road. Emma responds with some vague gesture and, visibly annoyed, immediately reshuts the window.

While her husband is at work, she mulls over her unhappiness. She is already beginning to ask herself why she ever bothered to get married. The words *"bliss, passion, ecstasy,"* over which she had often sighed, and which seemed so beautiful to her in her sentimental novels, now seem deceptive and meaningless.

Conjugal life becomes woven of complete predictability. Charles's conversation is "commonplace as a street pavement, and every one's ideas trooped through it in their everyday garb."

But the most grotesque thing of all is that Charles believes their marriage "happy." This certainty on his part cannot but raise such a blind rage in Emma's soul that she comes to loathe "this easy calm, this serene heaviness" of her young husband.

Even Charles's sexual "outbursts" had become predictably regular: "He embraced her at certain fixed times. It was one habit among other habits, like a familiar dessert after the monotony of dinner." That is, "ennui, the silent spider, was weaving its web in the darkness" of the Bovary household.

This boredom is broken by an unexpected surprise: an invitation to Vaubyessard, to a party at the castle of the Marquis of Andervilliers—an invitation that parts the fog of conjugal life like a ray of sun. Emma's yearning finally has something upon which to feed. The castle is luxurious, full of light and well-liveried servants. Emma gazes ecstatically at everything, tastes the delicacies she is served, and notes that she has never enjoyed such exquisite ices. Ordinary powdered sugar seems whiter and finer here than anywhere else.

The men there at the castle "had the complexion of wealth— that clear complexion that is heightened by the pallor of porcelain, the shimmer of satin, the veneer of old furniture, and that a well-ordered diet of exquisite food maintains at its best."

The Marquis of Andervilliers himself invites Emma to dance. Emma ecstatically abandons herself to it. Hence we discover her to be an expert dancer, charmingly swept up as she is in the arms of her elegant knight.

But on this occasion Flaubert again regards Emma with very little sympathy. While he calls our attention to her grace and beauty, he puts us on guard at the same time against her egotism, which can occasionally transform itself into cruel insensitivity, or even hurtful abuse.

In fact, when Charles, in his tenderly endearing timidity, also decides to take a turn at dancing, Emma blasts him with a ferociously reproachful glare. A doctor who commands respect, she hisses at him, does not leap into the midst of the dancers. Mortified, he returns downcast to his seat, not daring to contradict her.

Charles will later approach Emma with an affectionate gesture, pleased that she is enjoying herself and wearing such a happy expression. But Emma barely acknowledges him and brutally brushes him off, saying, "'Don't touch me! . . . I'll be all rumpled.'"

After returning home, Emma predictably falls back into her previous state of boredom. The visit to the Marquis and Marquise of Andervilliers has left a "gap in her life, like the huge crevasses that a thunderstorm will sometimes carve in the mountain, in the course of a single night."

Her gown has been put back into the armoire together with her satin shoes, "whose soles were yellowed with the slippery wax of the dancing floor. Her heart resembled them: in its contact with wealth, something had rubbed off on it that could not be removed."

To console herself, Emma buys a street map of Paris, and traces with the tip of her finger various imaginary strolls through the capital. At the same time, she subscribes to various ladies' magazines with promising names like *La Corbeille* (the basket) and *Sylphe des Salons* (the sylph of the salons).

Flaubert was extremely scrupulous and gathered much information before writing: "For two days now I have been trying to enter into the dreams of young girls," he writes in a letter to his lover, Louise Colet, on March 3, 1852, "and for this purpose I have been navigating in milky oceans of books about castles and troubadours in white-plumed velvet hats. . . . You can give me the exact details that I need." The suggestion illustrates Flaubert's subtle treachery, as if he were saying: only you who are so knowledgeable about trivial things in poor taste can give me some ideas about Emma's choices.

And again to Louise: "I have to place my heroine in a ball. But it has been so long since I have seen one that it will require a huge effort of imagination. And yet it is such a common thing, so often spoken and respoken of everywhere. It will be amazing if I manage to avoid triviality, and yet I do want to avoid it."

Emma cannot live without following, if only from afar, "all the accounts of first nights, races, and soirées, . . . the debut of a singer, . . . the opening of a new shop."

Not having anything to say to her husband, she reaches the point of bringing the book or magazine she is reading to the table so she can casually page through it while Charles eats, chatting on by himself.

"The nearer things were the more her thought turned away from them," Flaubert explains to us; "All her immediate surroundings, the wearisome countryside, the petty-bourgeois stupidity, the mediocrity of existence seemed to her the exception, an exception in which she had been caught by a stroke of fate, while beyond stretched as far as eye could see an immense land of joys and passions."

Emma confuses, in her desire, "the sensuous pleasures of luxury with the delights of the heart, elegance of manners with delicacy of sentiment."

How better can one describe the anguish of a heart incapable of love, rank with boredom? At certain times this boredom of Emma's greatly resembles that of her author, as it is described in his letters. "I am bored with life, with myself, with others, with everything. By sheer strength of will I have managed to form the habit of work. But when I've taken a break from work, all that boredom floats back up to the surface like a swollen carcass, its green belly sticking up, polluting the air that I breathe" (December 2, 1846).

Or: "What a sad, sad Sunday I spent yesterday. . . . You are happy," he wrote to Louise Colet on September 14, 1846; "You are not nauseated by boredom which makes you wish for death. You don't carry within yourself the boredom of life."

Emma is waiting for something to happen, something which will distract her from the unbearable monotony of marriage. Another invitation to Vaubyessard from the Marquis of Andervilliers? Maybe. But maybe also something else. But what? Meanwhile, the gray days passed one by one, all the same, and she who from the beginning was in the habit when alone of sitting down at the piano now asked herself, "What was the good of playing? Who would hear her?" And so, ever more frequently, the piano remained silent.

Emma quits reading her romance novels. Little by little she lets herself go, even physically. She no longer bothers with the housework or with her toilet. She spends entire days in her bedroom wrapped in her robe, wearing "grey cotton stockings." She becomes capricious and unpredictable, "one day drank only pure milk, and the next cups of tea by the dozen."

Why the others and not her? This is the thought which disturbs her. "She had seen duchesses at Vaubyessard with clumsier waists and commoner ways" than hers. Why did the Marquise possess horses and servants, while Emma has to content herself with this provincial backwater? "She hated the divine injustice of God," who had deprived her of everything, leaving her only the awareness of her eternally unsatisfied appetites.

Aren't these also the rancorous sentiments of the wretched Demon of Sologub?[1] Between him and Emma there are certain similarities; they are in some sense cousins. But while Sologub presents his hero as overtly contemptible and distant from himself, Flaubert writes of his Emma as of a creature who is indeed vile but also beloved or, at the very least, tolerated—too deeply sympathized with and abhorred not to have been in some way an influence on him. So much so, perhaps, that he confuses himself with her, believes himself her brother, her equal.

Emma is overwhelmed by envy, like the wretched Demon, but does nothing to satisfy her greedy desire. "She leant her head against the walls to weep; she longed for lives of adventure, for masked balls, for shameless pleasures that were bound, she thought, to initiate her to ecstacies she had not yet experienced."

She becomes pale and begins to suffer from palpitations. Her husband, always solicitous and adoring, administers valerian drops to her and prescribes camphor baths. But everything he tried to do for her "only seemed to irritate her the more."

One of her little secret pleasures was to douse her arms with half a bottle of cologne.

Charles begins to believe that it is the unhealthful influence of the place where they live that is provoking this effect in her. He asks himself whether it would not be better if they moved elsewhere. In the meantime, Emma has adopted the habit of drinking vinegar to lose weight, and she has "contracted a sharp little cough, and lost all appetite."

1. Feodor Sologub, pseudonym of Feodor Kuzmich Teternikov, author of *The Little Demon* (1907).

When Charles and Emma Bovary depart from Tostes, Emma is pregnant. But it is not this new development which excites her so much as the idea of a change of whatever sort: new faces, a new house, and who knows what kinds of potential encounters, however vague and literary they yet appear to her imagination.

For the young doctor, this change of locale constitutes a serious setback. He will lose the few patients he has, with difficulty, accumulated. He will have to start from scratch. But his love for his wife is generous and free of doubts: if those surroundings make her sick, we will go someplace else. One's occupation and one's career come after the peace of mind and health of one's beloved. By chance, Charles finds a position eight leagues from Rouen, hence a place much less isolated and lonely than Tostes.

In Yonville, while waiting to settle into a new house, they take some rooms in an inn. They encounter there a young man, blond and fine-featured, who immediately attracts Emma's attention. His name is Léon, and he works as a clerk in a notary's office.

We are on the verge here of reaching the kernel of the novel's main theme: adultery. What does Flaubert think of it? The answer is elusive. On the one hand, he seems disgusted by the bourgeois Catholic demonization of female adultery. What is the harm, he seems to think, of a beautiful young woman, badly married to an inept and unsensual man and consumed by boredom, dreaming of love, finally realizing that dream when the right opportunity presents itself?

On the other hand, however, Flaubert seems fed up with the theme before even beginning to speak of it, as well as with the similarly unbearable rhetoric of lovers who confuse their navels with the universe and dress up their sexual desire in pretentious and high-flown phrases.

Charles Bovary has all the characteristics of a husband who, though excluding the unforeseen or any hint of sexual discord from his idea of married life, nevertheless admits the possibility of his wife's infidelity, even if only unconsciously.

He can admit such a possibility, that is, providing he finds nothing out—as his blind and at times even comic tolerance of the situation seems to suggest—providing he is not forced to choose!

Charles knows he is boring and something less than desirable. But he also knows that he does not want to lose the wife whom he loves. His idea of marriage is as simple and lazy as his character; he can be happy with very little and can see roses where there are only thorns.

But even here, Charles Bovary is treated by Flaubert with hidden sympathy, though he still calls him an idiot every five minutes. The reasons for Flaubert's indulgence toward Charles plumb the great depths of love. If Charles sins by unworthiness, he is never motivated by self-pity or profit seeking. He is truly generous, because he sincerely cares for the one he loves. He loves Emma so much that he does not see her mistakes, her impatience, her lies. His is a maternal love, unconscious and absolute, that tends to mask, to justify, to protect his beloved as though she were a favorite daughter.

And Emma? Emma, who at the beginning seems to elicit the author's solidarity, even moving him to justify the most secret desires, the most profound longings of his character—Emma, whose desire to flee seems to be exculpated by the pedestrian gawkiness of her husband, by the tedium of a provincial life with no escape, by her peculiar sensitivity to the beautiful—what does Emma think and feel in the eyes of her author?

This is where Flaubert accomplishes his miracle: justifying adultery while condemning the adulteress, understanding what makes a life impoverished and boring while fiercely condemning the one who is incapable of turning that life to good account, the one who, like Emma, feeds instead upon fatuous literature and impossible dreams.

Flaubert, that is, does the exact opposite of the Catholic Church, which condemns the sin and pardons the sinner, strictly judging the transgression of the law while granting lenience to the individual transgressor. The sinner then humbly acknowledges guilt, perhaps to sin again later, while the law remains intact.

If there is something to condemn in the act of adultery, Flaubert wants us to see, it is not the sin of the flesh but, rather, a lack of imagination, hypocritical behavior made up of little subterfuges and sinister lies.

The author expresses these same feelings in life as well as art.

It is not the adultery of Louise Colet—who, while married to Hippolyte Colet, nevertheless chose her lovers at will—that roused Flaubert's indignation. What he hated was that she let her romantic choices be dictated by her affected and slightly naive admiration for fashionable writers and philosophers rather than by any real sensual attraction.

On the other hand, Flaubert himself was hardly the type to confront the truth where his own affections were concerned. He took pains his whole life to hide his feelings for other women from his mother, and did so unhesitatingly, using lies, subterfuge, and the most overt forms of deception.

But let us return to Emma, who, sitting before the fire in the inn that first night in Yonville, chats away the evening with the young clerk. It is a happy moment for her, caught up as she is in the novel pleasure of being discreetly courted by Léon, and caught up as well in her pregnancy, which is accompanied by her usual self-deluding fantasies. It would be a boy, she tells herself, "he would be strong and dark." He would be special, a cherub; "she would call him George," and he would take upon himself and avenge all that she has suffered.

But Emma, Flaubert tells us, is incapable of being satisfied. Her nature, complicated by her training within a culture of systematic mystification, always leads her to desire something else, something distant, unreachable, fictitious.

Such a personality, however, also belongs in part to her author, as we discover from Flaubert's letters. The present is repugnant to him as well, almost as if he is watching the present transform itself into the past as he lives it. He, too, while enjoying one thing, covets another.

We recognize ourselves, at least to some extent, in such very human feelings. But Flaubert is vexed by them, sorely so, as if they were something in him to condemn, even if at other times he seems nevertheless to indulge himself in them. In a letter to Louise he writes: "Ten years seem to have passed since we were last in Mantes. It is distant, so distant this memory: it already appears to me in a splendid and sad distance, shimmering in a vague color both bitter and passionate. It is as beautiful, in my head, as a sunset upon the snow. My life is all snow right now; the sun that beats upon it is this memory; the red reflection is the ember that illuminates it" (September 14, 1846).

Emma truly seems to form part of Flaubert's mental structure. She, however, is blamed for not being able to examine and judge herself as he does, for not being able to build an original verbal architecture out of her weaknesses that redeems their disorder. Emma feeds on mediocre books, and therefore her dissatisfactions are never truly tragic, just grotesque, not to be pitied but derided.

"A man, at least, is free," Emma says, "He can explore all passions and all countries, overcome obstacles, taste of the most distant pleasures. But a woman is always hampered. Being inert as well as pliable, she has against her the weakness of the flesh and the inequity of the law. Like the veil held to her hat by a ribbon, her will flutters in every breeze; she is always drawn by some desire, restrained by some rule of conduct."

It seems as if we are listening to the sentiments of Louise Colet, the woman Flaubert loved for some months with a surprised and passionate love and with whom he continued to correspond for fully six years (from 1846 to 1848, and then again from 1851 to the beginning of 1855)—desiring her and rejecting her, flattering her and offending her, the whole time.

Louise was a beautiful woman ten years older than Flaubert. When they met, he was twenty-five and she thirty-five. She had full blonde hair and wore a blue dress, very similar if not identical to the blue merino dress that Emma Bovary is wearing when Charles meets and falls in love with her. She was a generous woman, intelligent, outgoing, sensitive, and full of mistaken ambitions.

I say "mistaken" because her writings (verses, comedies, and novels) are pompous and devoid of originality, yet Louise wanted to think of herself as more creative than George Sand and Madame de Lafayette combined. She had no ear for written language, even though many of her verses are certainly more than respectable and her book about farm women, *La Paysanne*, is a work of great ambition and passion.

What Flaubert detested in Louise was a certain "social optimism" that led her to throw herself into lost causes with quixotic fervor. It was Louise who, inspired by the memory of Jean Baptiste

Le Blanc, her famous revolutionary grandfather, wanted to travel to Italy to meet Garibaldi, admirably and courageously willing to brave the cannon fire. And it was Louise who, risking arrest, went to London to speak to Mazzini, while Flaubert spent his vacations in pursuit of some juicy (and at times empty) dream of a depraved and mystical Orient.

We need only remember the visions of deserts, camels, plumes, and palm trees which recur in so many of his letters. When Flaubert does decide to travel to his fantastic Orient, he is disappointed, though nonetheless excited by it. His rendezvous with the famous priestess and prostitute Kuchuk-Hânem gets him a case of syphilis so bad that when he returns to Croisset his mother barely recognizes him: he is losing his hair, has gained weight, and has been relieved of the better part of his teeth.

Flaubert, moreover, accuses Louise of "imprecision" in writing. He who was so precise and punctilious could not stand her amateurishness: "Six stories in ten days. I don't understand. . . . I'm like an old aqueduct: so much slag encrusts the walls of my brain that thought flows through it extremely slowly, dripping from my pen drop by drop" (November 29, 1853).

We know that for Flaubert writing was "labor"; we know that he could take days, months, to search for a word, a turn of phrase. The Goncourt brothers often ridiculed him for this in their diaries, saying that for Flaubert rhythm was "an idolatry" (April 1861). And again: "You know, the poor fellow has one remorse that is poisoning his life. . . . It's that, in *Madame Bovary*, he stuck two genitives one right on top of the other" (March 3, 1862).[2]

On the other hand, Flaubert himself declared that he was a "prisoner" of the style that tortured and tormented him. "Comparisons consume me like flies, and I spend my whole time squashing them; my sentences are swarming with them" (December 27, 1852).

Or again: "(I am sure of one thing: no one has ever conceived a more perfect type of prose than I; but as to the execution, how weak, how weak, oh God!) Nor does it seem to me impossible to give psychological analysis the swiftness, clarity, and impetus of a strictly dramatic narrative. That has never been attempted, and

2. *The Goncourt Journals, 1851–1870*, ed. and trans. Lewis Galantière (Garden City, N.Y.: Doubleday, Doran, & Co., 1937), 114–15.

it would be beautiful. Have I succeeded a little in this? I have no idea. At this moment I have no definite opinion about my work" (July 22, 1852).

"I have a rheumatism in my neck these days that gives me a rather ridiculous appearance. But this would be a small matter if not for the suffering my style causes; it troubles me more than all the other sicknesses in the world. For three and a half months I have been writing from sunrise to sunset without interruption. I have reached the point of permanent irritation, in this incessant impossibility to 'vomit' in which I find myself. Whatever the bourgeois may say, this whipped cream is not so easy to whip. The further along I get, the more difficult it becomes to write the simplest things, and the more emptiness I find in the things I had judged to be the best" (end of November, 1847).

Louise, in the meantime, in addition to the continual gifts (gloves, a ring, walking sticks—things that perfectly suit Emma's taste, we will discover), sends Flaubert books that she has loved: Madame de Girardin's *Cléopâtre*, for example (which he character-izes as "a vile hash"), Lamartine's *Graziella*, and other fashionable books.

"Yes, there are some charming details," he says of Lamartine, responding to Louise's insistence, "two or three pretty nature im-ages that flash out occasionally like the wink of an eye, but that's all. And frankly, does he screw her or not? . . . How beautiful these love stories are in which the essential thing is so shrouded in mys-tery that one doesn't know what to think, sexual intercourse being systematically relegated to the shadows, as are eating, drinking, pissing, etc." (April 24, 1852).

From ridicule, however, Flaubert goes on to patient advice: "Don't overlook anything, work, rework, and don't abandon the task until you feel convinced that you have brought the work to the furthest point of perfection that was possible" (end of No-vember, 1847).

As one might do with a schoolteacher, Louise sends Flaubert her writings to correct. With infinite patience, he passes entire afternoons parsing the rhymes of his disciple, heavily marking her manuscripts. "Here is the finished work [*The Acropolis of Athens*]. We've been at it from two on, without a break, save for an hour to

29

dine. I have great hopes. It will work fine. We have made your work easy for you. . . . Bouilhet is searching right now for the final line. He was sublime. . . . The whole piece was entirely reworked by him. And he has had an idea that I would dare call Dantean and monumental. . . . And now, to repay us for our work, which was by no means mediocre, have this immediately recopied (for yourself and for us) exactly the way we've corrected and reworked it[,] . . . and then we will see if there is anything left to rewrite. The whole piece will then be more clearly visible. . . . The verses with dirty faces have had them washed, and the rabble of mediocre ones has been pitilessly cast out" (March 14, 1853).

When Louise protests that she can no longer recognize her verses, Flaubert replies: "When a line was bad we agonized over how to improve it, but did not completely change it so it would mesh with the one that followed, which we preserved as it stood. . . . We doggedly labored to remove bad assonances, re-work apostrophes and stresses (something you don't pay enough attention to), and didn't assume the final effect had been achieved, only approximated. We called your attention to passages that were clearly badly executed. . . . So for example, in place of this line, '*La colonnade encore debout des Propylées*,' we substituted, '*L'eternelle blancheur des longues Propylées*.' It seems we were not mistaken. . . . There were passages on which Bouilhet and I could not agree, so we left them alone for fear of making further errors. And as for the other pieces, we always spontaneously exclaimed together: 'no, no, this one we will not let her get away with'" (March 14, 1853).

But Louise was not happy. She fought back, defending her verses as they were written. Flaubert responded with annoyance to her complaints. For example, on March 11, 1853, he replied: "My first instinct was to send you back your manuscript without a word, since our observations are of no use to you, and since you don't want to (or cannot) listen to reason. To what end do you ask us our opinion and then give us a hard time, if the only thing that comes of it is wasted time and recriminations on both sides? I confess that if I did not control myself, I would give you a further piece of my mind, and that this fact makes me feel a great sadness: how am I supposed to regard your adulatory judgments of my work when I then see that you make such gross errors in yours? If you

30

did it to defend the eccentricities, the original qualities, and so on, fine! But no, it is always banalities that you defend, nonsense that is harmful to your thought, bad assonances and trite turns of phrase. You insist upon trifles. When I tell you that '*sardoine*' is the French word for '*sardonix*,' which is Latin, you reply that it makes you think of 'sardine.'. . . Ah, if you had written *Melaenis*, then we would have had substantial matter for discussion. In your frenzy to correct our corrections you add only errors. The *silk* umbrella. The Greeks had no knowledge of silk, or it was so rare that it was as if they had no knowledge of it." Of a story about a woman who dies in the arms of her rapist, Flaubert indignantly writes: "No, one cannot write like this! It is inappropriate and indecent. . . . Moreover, where is the raped woman who ever died of it?" In comments such as these, Flaubert combines a certain male arrogance with his psychological and stylistic tutelage.

This letter reveals a most strange situation: Louise Colet, Flaubert's beloved, lives at a distance from him and is harshly scolded by her lover for her way of writing, whereas Louis Bouilhet and Flaubert are together in Croisset, spending hours editing her texts and mixing their severe professionalism with comradely cruelty. You can almost see them bent over the manuscript pages, relentlessly digging through Louise's somewhat maladroit verses to "make her pay."

What seems hard to understand, however, is Louise's blindness. How could she not have felt the malevolence of the two friends who made fun of her behind her back and then at the earliest opportunity wrote scathingly of her? While it is true they never reveal their antics to her overtly, their letters contain hints of an attitude which, however obscurely expressed, is nevertheless perfectly recognizable.

"Have you roused your monstrous motor to action? (motor = engine of war, instrument of pleasure)," Flaubert writes to Louis Bouilhet. "Upon Edma or upon la Blanchecotte? Or upon both of them? No matter, you have no beauties in your harem (though it's true they are both a bit appetizing). . . . That Blanchecotte woman will probably be a pest. She is a hot-head, be careful. . . . It would certainly be wiser to resort to the old masturbation. . . . You are forgetting Ludovica: it would be a mistake not to see her, she is one

31

who can make you discharge your weapon better than the Muse [Louise Colet], *inter nos.* While we are on the subject, let us talk about her. You know that in her letter before last she insinuated and even outright said that you could leave me before long, or at least 'prefer other friends one day,' and she sang great praises of Guérard whom you would love 'more each day' because he at least would concern himself with the 'stuff of life'? (I beg you not to say a word of any of this!) I was so indignant that I had to restrain myself from writing back. I would have replied too hurtfully. I found the slyness of her rhetoric entirely too obvious. And if she were saying all of this in good faith, poor woman? . . . I only put her in her place a bit, humorously, that's all. But what do you think of this horse's ass of a woman who tries to put herself between us two? . . . She grieves me greatly this poor Muse. I don't know what to do about it. . . . How do you think this will all end? I feel that she is tired of me. For her own peace of mind let us hope she leaves me. She is a twenty-year-old from the point of view of the emotions and I am sixty (you should study us a bit, on this point)" (December 8, 1853).

But Louise, like Emma, has a talent for not seeing things. She did not see and did not understand that her Gustave, not having the courage himself to leave her, was bored to tears and hoped that she would be the one to take the initiative. She did not see that the two men shared an intimacy which excluded her, notwithstanding the complex epistolary relationship between the three.

"You love me tremendously," Gustave writes to Louise on December 14, 1853, "much more than I have ever been loved or ever shall be. But you love me as anyone else might, with the same preoccupation with secondary concerns and the same incessant worries. . . . You get irritated over a change of my locale, over a departure, over an acquaintance to whom I pay a visit, and you believe that this bothers me? No, no. This pains and disheartens me on your behalf. . . . Listen to Bouilhet. He is a great man who not only knows how to write verse but possesses good sense, as the bourgeois say, a thing the bourgeois usually lack — not to mention poets."

"You cry when you are alone, poor friend. But no, don't cry; evoke the company of the works to be created; think back to the eternal figures. . . . Men, in effect, always want to be loved, even when they themselves do not love at all, and I have sometimes wished you loved me less; I did so in moments when I loved you the most, when I saw you suffering because of me" (November 29, 1853).

"You are in love with life; you are a pagan and a southerner; you believe in the passions and hope for happiness. . . . But I loathe life. I am a Catholic with something of the green effluence of Norman cathedrals in my heart. . . . How can you expect a man as besotted with Art as I am, perpetually hungry for an ideal he never attains[,] . . . how can you expect such a man to love with the heart of a twenty-year-old, and with the *ingenuous* passions proper to that age?" (December 14, 1853).

"Curses upon the family that softens the heart of the courageous, that urges every cowardice and every concession, that drowns us in oceans of milk and tears!" (October 5, 1855).

How much more clearly could Flaubert have expressed his repugnance for romantic custom, for every prolonged attachment, for every institutionalization of love?

The women to whom Flaubert was attracted were either prostitutes (how often we find him happy in bordellos with his friends!) or married women, with whom he could exchange only the occasional clandestine word, as he apparently did with Elisa Schlésinger in Trouville.

Louise Colet was the one who provided the exception to the rule, whose arrival disrupted Flaubert's existence as a provincial bachelor. But she quickly came to bore him, and since she was neither prostitute nor clandestine adulteress, he was unable to brutally break off with her. Therefore the relationship dragged on, composed of occasional and sporadic encounters on neutral turf, neither his house in Croisset nor hers in Paris.

The emotional and spiritual life, the play of the senses, the exchange of ideas, these were things which took place elsewhere, in the company of his friends, the young men enamored of literature and of adventurous travel.

It is worth taking the trouble at this juncture to consider in its entirety a letter that was censored from the official *Correspondance* and that might help us understand Flaubert's impulse toward "androgyny."

"This morning, poor and dear old man," Flaubert wrote to Bouilhet on January 15, 1850, "I received your good and long letter so eagerly expected. It moved me to my very kidneys. How often I think of you, inestimable rogue! How many times a day do I think of you and mourn your absence. . . . Here I devote myself completely to the study of perfumes and the creation of unguents. . . . I often frequent the turkish baths. I devoured your verses from *Melaenis*. Let us pause, let us calm ourselves. He who knew not how to contain himself never learned how to write. I am bored to farting. I wish I could pummel your head with my fists. . . . We haven't yet had any dancing-girls; they are all in exile in Upper Egypt. The beautiful bordellos no longer exist, not even in Cairo. The party we were planning to have on the Nile the last time I wrote you didn't come off. However, nothing is lost. We have had male dancers. Oh! Oh! Oh! . . . As dancers, imagine two rascals, quite ugly, but charming in their corruption, in the deliberate degradation of their glances and the femininity of their movements, their eyes painted with antimony and dressed as women. For costume, they had loose trousers and an embroidered jacket. The latter came down to the epigastrium, whereas the trousers, held up by an enormous cashmere girdle folded double several times, began only at the bottom of the stomach, so that the entire stomach, the loins, and the beginning of the buttocks are naked, seen through a black gauze held tight against the skin by the upper and lower garments. At every movement, this gauze ripples with a mysterious, transparent undulation. The music never changed or stopped during the two hours. . . . A quivering of the muscles is the only way to describe it; when the pelvis moves, the rest of the body is motionless; when the breast shakes, nothing else moves. In this manner they advance toward you, their arms extended and rattling a kind of metal castanet, and their faces, under the rouge and the sweat, remain more expressionless than a statue's. By that I mean that they never smile. The effect is produced by the gravity of the head in contrast to the lascivious movements of the body. Sometimes they lie down flat on their backs, like a woman ready to be fucked, then rise up with a movement of the loins similar to that of a tree which swings back into place after the wind has stopped. In their bowings and salutations their great trousers suddenly inflate like oval balloons, then seem to melt away, expelling the air that swells them. From time to time, during the dance, the impresario who brought them plays around with them, kissing them on the stomach and the loins, and makes obscene remarks in an effort to put additional spice into a thing which is already quite clear in itself. It is too beautiful to be exciting. I doubt whether we shall find the women as good as the men; the ugliness of the latter adds greatly to the thing as Art. I had a headache for the rest of the day. . . . Here it is well accepted. People confess to their own sodomy; it is discussed at the dinner table. Occasionally one will deny it for a bit, but then everyone shouts you down, and so one winds up confessing after all. . . . Since we are traveling for our own education and we are conducting a mission for the government, we felt it was incumbent upon us to experience this mode of ejaculating. The occasion has not yet presented itself, but we are searching for it. It is at the baths that one finds it practiced. One makes a reservation for a bath (5 franks), including the masseurs, the pipe, the coffee, the linens, and they slip a boy of your own into one of the private rooms. . . . You know of course that all the boys of the baths are hustlers. These young masseurs are quite obliging. We [Flaubert and his traveling companion, Maxime Du Camp] spotted one in a bathing place very near our house. I had a bath reserved for myself alone. I went. The proprietor that afternoon was not around. . . . I was alone in the depths of the hot-room, watching the daylight fade through the great glass bull's-eyes in the dome. Hot water was flowing everywhere; stretched out indolently I thought of a quantity of things as my pores tranquilly dilated. It is very voluptuous and sweetly melancholy to take a bath like that quite alone. . . . The other day Maxime got screwed in the deserted quarter of the city among the ruins and enjoyed himself greatly. But enough of all this lubricity."

And Flaubert responded to Bouilhet, who had written from Paris a month or so later: "By the way, you ask me if I consummated that situation in that bath. Yes, and upon a vigorous young man with smallpox scars who wore an enormous white turban. It made me laugh, that's all. But I shall do it again. For an experience to come off well it must be reiterated. Farewell, old plumed one, to you now and forever; as Antony says, was he beautiful?" (June 2, 1850).

One Sunday morning, at about six, Emma gives birth. "'It is a girl!'" Charles happily tells her. But Emma does not even look at her: "She turned her head away and fainted."

The baby is named Berthe. After a few days, she is sent to a wet nurse, as was the custom, to a certain *mère* Rollet, a carpenter's wife, who lives in a poor and dirty house outside of Yonville. Louise Colet had done exactly the same, sending her newborn baby to a wet nurse far from home. On the other hand, so did all the wealthy mothers of that time.

It is not clear whether the antipathy Emma instinctively feels for her daughter is due to her resemblance to her father or to Emma's disappointment at having given birth to a girl rather than a boy, as she had dreamed: "He would be strong and dark; she would call him George."

A month later, while she is on the way to pay one of her rare visits to her daughter at the wet nurse's, she encounters the handsome Léon for the first time outside the inn. They bump into each other, and while he hems and haws, worried about compromising her, she begs him to accompany her to see the infant.

They walk together almost without speaking, full of emotion, each caught up in a private dream. But at the house of the wet nurse, reality will descend on them in all of its dreariness. "At the noise of the gate the wet nurse appeared with a baby she was suckling on one arm. With her other hand she was pulling along a poor puny little boy, his face covered with a scrofulous rash, the son of a Rouen hosier."

The woman lets them in, careless of the disorder in which she keeps the house. Emma's baby is sleeping on the floor in a wicker basket. Emma takes her in her arms and begins to gently rock her, softly singing a lullaby. Léon, in the meanwhile, walks back and forth in the house's only room, asking himself how it was possible that a beautiful woman dressed in silk should find herself in the midst of all that poverty.

The baby spits up on her mother's collar; irritated, Emma quickly puts her back into the basket on the floor. The wet nurse hurries to clean Emma up, reassuring her that the spot will not show. She then asks Madame Bovary to order her some soap, as she does not have enough money to buy it. "'All right, all right!'" Emma replies, "'Good-bye, Madame Rollet.'"

The wet nurse accompanies them to the door, complaining about how difficult it is to get up at night for the baby. Emma seems not to be listening to her, however. She is anxious to be off with her Léon, away from the dim, stinking room where she abandons her daughter without a single guilty feeling for leaving her in that condition.

But Léon is by her side: Léon has blond curls, well-manicured hands. His nails, too, are quite aristocratic, much longer than one generally finds in Yonville, Emma notes admiringly. One of the clerk's greatest concerns, in fact, as Flaubert maliciously points out, is tending his nails: "For this purpose he kept a special knife in his writing-desk."

For Flaubert, tending one's nails reveals the utmost degree of bourgeois vanity and self-satisfaction. Later on, we will see Emma judged quite harshly for her assiduous care of her own nails.

Léon and Emma walk slowly back to Yonville along the edge of the little stream which passes through the town. "While they forced themselves to find trivial phrases, they felt the same languor stealing over them both; it was like the deep, continuous murmur of the soul dominating that of their voices."

"A kind of bond" is established between Léon and Emma, "a constant exchange of books and of romances." It is implied that these are romances of poor quality, the kind of fashionable novels that Flaubert felt Louise Colet could have liked.

Naturally, Charles Bovary has no idea that anything is amiss. To the contrary, he is happy to see that his wife has taken up painting again, that she is eating better, that she has lost that persistent dry cough, and that of late she has even been more attentive and friendly to him.

If Charles's gaze, however blind, is tender and affectionate, Emma's for her husband is malevolent and cruel: "His cap was drawn down over his eyebrows, and his two thick lips were trembling, which added a look of stupidity to his face; his very back, his calm back, was irritating to behold, and she saw all his platitude spelled out right there, on his very coat."

Flaubert judgmentally describes the gaze which Emma turns upon the affectionate Charles as "a sort of depraved pleasure." The one she directs at Léon, however, is quite different: his blue eyes seemed to her "more limpid and more beautiful than those mountain-lakes which mirror the heavens."

At this perfect moment, Lheureux, the merchant of fine objects, enters upon the scene, fat, flabby, beardless, with a face that "seemed dyed by a decoction of liquorice."

"Polite to obsequiousness, he always held himself with bent back," while his mind was occupied with selling "Algerian scarves, . . . packages of English needles, a pair of straw slippers," and other delights.

Of "delights" such as these—which Flaubert treats with such disdain—we find traces in his letters, but described in very different tones. "I confess this weakness," he writes to Louise on September 14, 1846, telling her of having ordered some silk sashes from a merchant in Smyrna. "They are trivialities that for me are quite serious things. Farewell, I kiss the soles of your feet."

A month later, on October 13, he writes: "I received the silk sashes. I will bring you one. . . . Perhaps you can tie it in your hair the way they were doing two years ago with the Algerian hair nets. . . . You will see, and you can have it if you like."

In the novel, it will be Emma who is attracted to the small precious oriental objects, for which she will go into debt to the merchant Lheureux in order to possess.

In the meantime, Madame Bovary decides to take her daughter back from the wet nurse. She does this neither out of affection, nor out of remorse for having left her in those dirty, miserable surroundings, but simply because she suddenly feels a desire to play the part of the diligent and attentive mother.

Flaubert immediately puts us on guard against this new development: "She claimed to love children," he writes, "they were her consolation, her joy, her passion, and she accompanied her caresses with lyrical outbursts that would have reminded any one but the Yonvillians of Sachette in 'Notre Dame de Paris.'" It is as if Flaubert is saying: another performance, another literary model, another mystification.

The passage is also a satiric jab at Victor Hugo, so much admired by Louise, with whom a few years later Flaubert would initiate a clandestine correspondence. The letters to Hugo, exactly like those Louise wrote him, had to be sent to a certain address, have their envelopes changed, and be re-sent from there. With Hugo, however, these clandestine letters were not amorous but political. Hugo was living in exile in England, and writing to him was prohibited.

Louise, who had a weakness for great writers, had ferreted him out at his English hideaway and had created an elaborate network of communications going from her to Hugo, from Hugo to Flaubert, and from Flaubert, always through others, to Hugo.

"However full of bad writing" Flaubert thought Hugo, "he can still bury all the others. . . . What measure, what cadence!—I will hazard a theory here that I would never dare mention to anyone: great men often write very badly" (September 25, 1852).

Louise not only sought out great writers; she often became their lover. This was her generous and tactile way of living literature.

Her love affairs were tempestuous ones, and often, it must be admitted, her lovers proved inferior to her enthusiasms for them. The philosopher Victor Cousin was perhaps the most generous, the most faithful, and the most sympathetic. He constantly asked her to marry him and, dying, left her daughter a small inheritance.

Then there were Alfred de Musset, Alfred de Vigny, Champfleury, Charles Leconte de Lisle, Alphonse Daudet, and even Baudelaire, who attended her salon for a time—not to mention Victor Hugo, who wrote her letters that were more than affectionate. But Louise clearly wanted to make it known, and she writes as much in her *mémentos*, that the most beloved of them all was Flaubert.

Gustave's attitude to Louise's many lovers was by no means one of disapproval. "I confess I have never in my whole life been jealous." A passage from a letter of March 13, 1854 contains Flaubert's thoughts on possessiveness: "Where is the woman, the idea, the country, the ocean that one can possess, have for oneself, alone. Someone has always already been over those surfaces and within those depths of which you believe yourselves to be masters. If it was not the body, it was the shadow, the image of a body. A thousand fantasy adulterers meet under the kiss which gives you pleasure. I can believe a little in physical virginity, but moral, no. And in the true sense of the word we are all cuckolded; indeed, arch-cuckolded."

What irritates Flaubert about Louise's behavior is her neophyte's ingenuousness, her fanatical provincialism of the spirit, which exhibit themselves in her desire to collect famous men.

But even Louise, in all her enthusiasm, had some appreciation of the qualities of the men she so admired. She was one of the first to speak of the "extraordinary talent" of Flaubert's writings, even before they had been published. "He is a great artist," she writes on January 15, 1852, on one of the pages of her fragmentary and occasional diary which she called *mémentos*. And this was her estimation, notwithstanding the fact that Maxime Du Camp came repeatedly to her to speak ill of his best friend.

Flaubert had her read some fragments from *The Temptation of Saint Anthony*. She found them "beautiful." But Maxime Du Camp, whom Flaubert himself had put into contact with Louise so that he could share their friendship, writes her that "Gustave's book is worthless" and that he would be disconsolate if Flaubert insisted on having his work published in the *Revue de Paris* (which Maxime edited with Théophile Gautier) because Du Camp wouldn't know how to reply.

"And yet I love him," Louise writes in her diary. "Am I so sure of Maxime's superiority to Gustave? As far as the intellect is concerned, Gustave seems superior. But what is happening? I am totally confused. What influence does Maxime have over Gustave? Before Maxime went to see him in Croisset, Gustave wrote me such sweet letters. I am preyed upon by so many doubts, what anguish!" (November 18, 1851).

Finally, after so many unkindnesses, so many "distractions" (Flaubert had no idea of the poverty in which Louise struggled; she could not afford to buy her own shoes, yet she never asked her lover for a dime), she reflects to herself in her diary: "Now I understand Gustave perfectly, he loves me exclusively for himself, with profound egotism, in order to satisfy his senses and to read me his works. But for my pleasure, for my satisfaction, he scarcely cares" (December 24, 1851).

Flaubert had been very attracted to Louise's body, which at the beginning he had eagerly loved, then lost interest in. After two years of silence, he returned to look for her and to make love to her, though casually and indifferently.

But some powerful force that impelled him toward her had existed, however Flaubert sought to deny it.

"The smoothness of the skin of your naked body! . . . You are the only woman whom I have loved and whom I have possessed. Hitherto the women I chose, I chose merely for the purpose of satisfying desires aroused in me by others. You made me untrue to my system, to my heart, perhaps to my nature, which, incomplete in itself, always seeks the incomplete" (August 8, 1846).

"I think of you always," he writes Louise on August 9, 1846, the year his passion for her crested:

> I keep dreaming of your face, of your shoulders, of your white neck, of your smile, of your voice that's like a love-cry. . . . You came along, and with the mere touch of a fingertip you threw everything into confusion. The old dregs boiled up again; the lake of my heart began to churn. . . . I must love you to tell you this. Forget me if you can, tear your soul from your body with your two hands and trample on it, to destroy the traces of me that are in it. Come, don't be angry.
>
> No, I embrace you, I kiss you. I feel wild. Were you here, I'd bite you; I long to do so—I, whom women jeer at for my coldness—I, charitably supposed to be incapable of sex, so little have I indulged in it. . . . I'll be your desire, you'll be mine. . . . Oh! The beauty of your face, all pale and quivering beneath my kisses! But how cold I was! I did nothing but look at you; I was surprised, charmed. . . . Come, I'll take another look at your slippers. They are something I'll never give up; I think I love them as much as I do you. . . . They smell of verbena—and of you in a way that makes my heart swell.

At the same time, however, Flaubert was overwhelmed by fear of the intense feelings which had grown in him. "I wish we had never met," he writes on August 8, 1846, " . . . and yet the thought of you is never absent from my mind[,] . . . for every sensation that enters my soul turns there to bitterness, like wine poured into jars which have been used too often. . . . It is you who are a child, you who are fresh and new. . . . The grandeur of your love fills me with humility."

41

He tried to explain his reluctance, rationalize away his fear: "I have never seen a child without thinking it would grow old, nor a cradle without thinking of a grave. The sight of a naked woman makes me think of her skeleton. . . . If you were not to love me, I should die; but you do love me, and I am writing you to stop. . . . You tell me . . . to write you every day. . . . But the very idea that you want a letter every morning will prevent me from writing it. Let me love you in my own way, in the way that my nature demands. Let me continue to love you with—since you call it that—originality! Force me to do nothing, and I will do everything. Understand me, do not reproach me" (August 8, 1846).

Louise, however, who did nothing by half measures, would by no means just "let herself be loved." Rather, she would love him ferociously, tyrannically, tormenting him with continual demands for his affection, for his faithfulness, to the point of exasperating the already naturally impatient Flaubert.

Emma possesses many of the qualities Flaubert so loved and feared in Louise: the blind impetuosity, the impatient desire to live intensely, a certain wantonness in the sexual embrace: "She undressed brutally, ripping off the thin laces of her corset so violently that they would whistle round her hips like a gliding snake. She went on tiptoe, barefooted, to see once more that the door was locked, then with one movement, she would let her clothes fall at once to the ground—then, pale and serious, without a word, she would throw herself against his breast with a long shudder."

Such parallels extend also to the two women's literary tastes, so similar in their naive lack of critical spirit—even if Louise, who as a writer was certainly better versed in literary matters, read works of much higher caliber than Emma did.

In addition to similarities of character, there are also certain coincidences and similarities of biographical fact in Flaubert's novel which deeply offended Louise when the book was published. She had all the more reason since, during the second chapter of their love affair, he had spoken so frequently of the novel he was writing as if it had nothing to do with her but had apparently been plotting his "betrayal" all along. He had been spying on her.

The first example of such betrayal is the silver and agate cigarette case engraved with the words *Amor nel cor*. Louise had given it as a gift to Flaubert in the early days of their love, and he had accepted it with elaborate expressions of pleasure and reciprocated love. In the novel, a cigarette case engraved with the same words is transformed into a medallion and given by Emma to Rodolphe. The author represents it as a gift in the poorest of taste by a hare-brained lover.

Given her fiery character, Louise responded with restraint in a poem published in *Le Monde illustré* in January 1859:

The silver setting, finely chiseled,
Had enameled flowers and gold chasing;
On its stone was engraved the phrase *Amor nel cor*,
A Tuscan verse filled with secret emotion.

It was for him, for him whom she loved like a god,
For him, callous to all human sorrow, uncouth to women.
Alas, she was poor and had little to give,
But all gifts are sacred that incarnate a soul.

Well! In a novel of traveling-salesman style,
As nauseating as a toxic wind,
He mocked that gift in a flat-footed phrase,
Yet kept the fine agate seal.[3]

There was also a handkerchief stained with blood (from Louise's nose) that Gustave saved for years in a kind of altar in which he kept fetish objects that reminded him of their love: the slippers, the cigarette case, the portrait with the lock of hair, the letters, the ring, the handkerchief, and such. All of these items ultimately appear in the novel.

"What a good idea I had to take your slippers!" Flaubert writes to Louise on the evening of August 8, 1846, "If you only knew how I gaze at them! The spots of blood on the handkerchief yellow and fade, but is that their fault? . . . Thank you for the portrait; I will put it with the slippers."

"When night falls and I am alone," Flaubert confesses, "quite sure that I won't be disturbed, and that everyone around me is asleep, I open the drawer I spoke to you of, and I pull out of it my relics and spread them upon the table: the dear little slippers, the

3. This English translation of Louise Colet's untitled poem is taken from *Rage and Fire: A Life of Louise Colet*, by Francine du Plessix Gray (New York: Simon & Schuster, 1994), 278–79.

handkerchief, your hair, the little bag of your letters; I reread them, I touch them" (August 23, 1846).

In *Madame Bovary* we find Emma "becoming dreadfully sentimental. She had insisted on exchanging miniatures; handfuls of hair had been cut off, and now she was asking for a ring—a real wedding-ring, in token of eternal union."

We also find that, "besides the riding-crop with its silver-gilt top, Rodolphe had received a signet with the motto *Amor nel cor.*" The gifts humiliated him. He refused to accept any others. But Emma insisted, and Rodolphe ended up accepting them, privately judging her, as a result, to be tyrannical and intrusive.

But the similarities between Emma and Louise do not end there. Not only did both have an only daughter (Emma's Berthe and Louise's Henriette) toward whom Flaubert exhibited an often coldly critical attitude. Flaubert also makes many similar observations on their respective characters: on their flashes of unjustified anger, their sudden and excessive generosity, their absolute lack of frugality, their tendency to dream of impossible things, and their regal behavior (which covers their almost complete lack of financial or social standing). That "I want and I cannot" which belongs to Emma's by now proverbial character also, with some slight variation, formed part of the generous and impulsive nature of Louise.

꧁꧂

In the meanwhile, following the thread of Emma's story, we find her intent on performing not only the role of the good mother but that of the good wife as well, and at the precise moment at which she begins to betray her husband. She finds once again that she likes cultivating a public persona that earns her the respect of society. Her intentions, however, are far too evident for them to prove other than mannered and artificial to Flaubert's eyes. Charles, as usual, notices nothing.

Returning from work, chilled by the night air, he is happy to find "his slippers put to warm near the fire[,] . . . his waistcoat [that] now never wanted lining, nor his shirt buttons," his dinner prepared and laid out on the table by the mistress of the house. He is immediately ready to attribute all of these changes to the improvement in Emma's health.

"She was so sad and so calm, at once so gentle and so reserved, that near her one came under the spell of an icy charm, as we shudder in churches at the perfume of the flowers mingling with the cold of the marble."

Everyone in Yonville is enchanted with the young Madame Bovary. People say that "she would not be out of place in a sous-préfecture!" "The housewives admired her thrift, the patients her politeness, the poor her charity."

But, to be sure, there is no reason whatsoever to think that there is the least bit of sincerity in any of Emma's actions. "She was eaten up with desires," Flaubert hurries to explain to us, "with rage, with hate," even if her "chaste lips never spoke" what was in her "tormented heart."

The fact is that Emma is in love with Léon but does not dare admit it to herself. She withdraws into solitude so that she can "more easily delight in his image." The more she realizes she loves him, the more she denies this love. What makes her resist, however, is not modesty or loyalty to her husband but, as her author tells us, "idleness and fear."

She sits before the mirror and repeats "I am virtuous" to herself, "striking resigned poses [which] consoled her a little for the sacrifice she thought she was making."

Furthermore, the fact that her husband gives no sign of recognizing her sufferings vexes her greatly. "His conviction that he was making her happy looked to her a stupid insult." Was he not himself "the obstacle to all happiness, the cause of all misery"? "Domestic mediocrity urged her on to wild extravagance, matrimonial tenderness to adulterous desires." "She would have liked Charles to beat her, that she might have a better right to hate him, to revenge herself upon him."

On rare occasions she becomes disgusted with and "loathe[s] this hypocrisy." She dreams of escaping somewhere with Léon to "try a new life," but immediately "a dark shapeless chasm would open within her soul."

At one point, Emma decides to go see a priest; maybe he will understand and will give her some good advice. But the Abbé Bournisien does not understand her request. "'And how are you?'" he asks her. "'Not well,'" she replies, "'I am suffering.'" "'So do I,'" he quickly returns, "'The first heat of the year is hard to bear, isn't it?'" He then asks her if her husband cannot administer some kind of medicine. "'He!'" she replies, then adds, "'It is no earthly remedy I need. . . . I should like to know . . .'" But the priest's attention is distracted by some boys who are fighting. She makes a final attempt to be heard, to be understood, but he has no time for the woman, preoccupied as he is with the problem of a cow, believed to be cursed, that he has been asked to cure. The priest, for his own part, simply cannot conceive how one who is *"bien chauffé et bien nourri"* could be suffering.

This is one of the most humorous scenes in the novel. It is a comic dialogue ready to be performed on stage. The brief interchange between Emma and the Reverend Bournisien captures the total lack of understanding that exists between two classes, two mind-sets, two religions (hers pagan, his humbly Christian), two cultures, two genders. They are both made fun of, but Flaubert has a greater appreciation for the priest, who has his feet firmly on the ground and his head on straight, than for the young woman, whose foolish and arrogant pretenses outweigh her sufferings, however real and painful they may appear to her.

Returning home, Emma sees her daughter, who, tottering on her weak little legs, comes to meet her; she roughly shoos her away, "pushing her back with one hand."

Undaunted, the little girl returns and hugs her mother's knees. "She looked up with her large blue eyes, while a small thread of clear saliva drooled from her lips on to the silk of [Emma's] apron." "'Leave me alone,'" the mother shouts "quite angrily." Her face is so contorted that it makes the little girl start to cry. But she tries one more time, timidly, to approach her mother, making Emma burst out with another "'leave me alone.'" She pushes her daughter furiously, sending her careening into a brass handle on a chest of drawers, which cuts her cheek. Blood flows from the wound. Emma becomes alarmed. "Madame Bovary rushed to lift her up, broke the bell-rope, called for the maid with all her might," and began to "curse herself."

Finally, thinks the reader, a spontaneous feeling of remorse, something immediate and sincere. But this seeming sincerity is quickly belied by Emma's actions. Turning toward her husband— who, having heard his daughter's screams, enters at that moment— Emma coldly says, "'Look, dear! . . . the child fell down while she was playing, and she hurt herself.'"

The scene is described in a way which displays how revolting the behavior of the young mother is. Not only does she throw her daughter, who had affectionately approached her, to the ground— so roughly, in fact, that she injures her—but rather than reproaching herself for her action, she immediately tells her husband that the little girl hurt herself, making her accusation with the dispassionate, controlled tone of one completely devoid of any moral sense.

The episode doesn't end there, however. Feeling uneasy, Emma does not go down to dinner with her husband. She remains near her child. And again the reader thinks that perhaps Emma has realized the error of her ways, perhaps she is truly sorry, perhaps some trace of humanity exists within this woman after all.

But Flaubert immediately destroys that hope. Seated beside her child, the mother revolves thoughts which are by no means affectionate but, rather, sordid and cruel: "The little anxiety she still felt gradually wore off, and she seemed very stupid to herself, and very kind to have been so worried just now at so little. Berthe, in fact, no longer cried. Her breathing now imperceptibly raised the cotton covering. Big tears lay in the corner of the half-closed eyelids, through whose lashes one could see two pale sunken pupils; the adhesive plaster on her cheek pulled the skin aside."

She casts a cold, hostile gaze on her daughter, its coldness joined by this far from maternal thought: "'It is very strange . . . how ugly this child is!'"

Meanwhile, the young clerk Léon, tired of loving with nothing to show for it, decides to leave the city. If Emma has not yet "yielded" to him (as one used to say), it is not to protect her virtue, Flaubert wants us to understand; it is because she so obstinately insists on performing the role of the good wife that she cannot disentangle herself from it. But despite her performance, dissatisfaction and hate still reign in her heart.

Léon departs, and a period of "bleakness" begins for Emma. "Sorrow blew into her soul with gentle moans, as the winter wind makes in ruined castles."

In her memory, Léon appears taller, more handsome, more charming. She obviously regrets not having loved him more freely. "She thirsted for his lips. She wanted to run after him, to throw herself into his arms and say to him, 'It is I; I am yours.'" But at the same time, she was prevented from doing so by "the difficulties of the enterprise, and her desires, increased by regret, became only the more acute."

Ultimately, however, "the flames subsided[,] . . . either because the supply had exhausted itself, or because it had been piled up too much." Her love died little by little beneath the pall of habit, "and the bright fire that had empurpled her pale sky was overspread and faded by degrees."

In her drowsy conscience, "she took her disgust for her husband for aspirations towards her lover, the burning of hate for the warmth of tenderness; but as the tempest still raged, and as passion burnt itself down to the very cinders, and no help came, no sun rose, there was night on all sides, and she was lost in the terrible cold that pierced her through."

To console herself, she indulges in purchases that satisfy her vanity: a gothic prie-dieu of expensive wood, antique vases, a silk dressing gown—this, at a time when she cannot find enough money to pay the housekeeper. Emma "in a month spent fourteen francs on lemons for polishing her nails," Flaubert emphasizes.

He had originally written "twenty-five francs a month on lemons for her nails." But the phrase had been edited by Maxime Du Camp; in a letter sent to Flaubert on October 14, 1856, he writes: "Twenty-five francs a month on lemons? The biggest lemons cost only five *sous:* doesn't a hundred lemons for one's nails seem a bit exaggerated, even for Yonville?" And Flaubert judiciously corrects the phrase.

Flaubert continues: "She wrote to Rouen for a blue cashmere gown." The detail reminds us that blue is Emma's, as well as Louise's, favorite color. In addition, "she chose one of Lheureux's finest scarves, and wore it knotted round her waist over her dressing-gown; thus dressed, she lay stretched out on the couch with closed blinds."

Can Lheureux's scarves be the famous silk sashes that the young Flaubert was having sent from Smyrna? The Flaubert household was also short of money, and after the death of Flaubert's father, the family was forced to economize in order to survive.

Even Emma's hairstyle no longer satisfies her. She begins to do her hair "*à la Chinoise,* in flowing curls, in plaited coils; she parted it on one side and rolled it under, like a man's."

We know how much this masculine hairstyling appealed to Flaubert's erotic tastes. As if out of spite or as an act of sexual pride, Emma, who has a delicately feminine body, sometimes wears some masculine object: curled hair, a hunter's vest, turkish pants, pincenez, a feathered cap.

And if, for Flaubert, these masculine touches impart a kind of perverse fascination to the soft body of the young woman, they become evidence, on the other hand, of a profound lack of internal stability.

Flaubert was certainly attracted to traces of masculinity in the female body. His letters to Louise Colet are full of such references. "What I want, in short, is that, like a new kind of hermaphrodite, you give me with your body all the joys of the flesh and with your mind all those of the soul" (September 28, 1846).

And again on that same day: "What you dislike, perhaps, is precisely the fact that I treat you as a man and not as a woman. Try to put some of your intelligence into your relations with me. Later your heart will thank your mind for this. I thought at first that I would find in you less feminine personality, a broader conception of life; but no! The heart, the heart! The poor heart, so kind, so charming, with its eternal graces, is always there, even in those women who are noblest and greatest."

And on April 12, 1854: "I have always tried (but it seems I've failed) to make a sublime hermaphrodite out of you. I want you to be a man from your head to your waist. Going down lower, you burden me and excite me and you are ruined by the feminine element."

After his relationship with Louise ended, Flaubert maintained a long correspondence with George Sand, who notoriously walked the streets of Paris dressed as a man. In *The Family Idiot*, Sartre speaks of an inherent feminine tendency that exists in Flaubert and in his erotic and literary choices.

Emma's decking herself out as a man, however, is seen as a sign of something more than mere braggadocio. Even here, Flaubert seems to tell us, she is typically capricious and volatile. She lacks the courage to follow her choices through, preferring instead to merely play her charade, allusively, flirtatiously, while avoiding any real consequences.

For Emma, the signs of a masculine "spirit" are merely another representation, because they correspond to nothing in her that Flaubert would call "a broader conception of life." For George Sand, on the other hand, such signs are accompanied by a real revolt against the conventions of gender.

Emma is like Louise, completely lacking in judgment and the capacity to reflect. When she believes she is being thoughtful, she is simply trying to rationalize her most immediate interests; she is absolutely incapable of the kind of impartiality to which "the heart" should be most indebted. So too is Louise's heart, with its "eternal graces," its sudden generosities, its pompous sincerity; she too was condemned to a stubborn, repetitious, inexorable femininity and to a life that recognized itself only in "winged" sentiments and maternal possessiveness.

And yet Flaubert loved Louise Colet, not George Sand, even

though he fled the first and sent the second admiring letters that begin with the words "Dear Master."

It is as if Flaubert's error consisted in the mere act of loving Louise, in consciously submitting to the eternal "deception" of the female body as such.

Emma, Flaubert seems to tell us, is loveable precisely because of her inability to form a more universal "conception of life," but she is unworthy, at the same time, for that very same lack, because her heart is blind and her hermaphroditic pretenses do not correspond to a real "cultivation of the free spirit," such as he will recognize in George Sand.

❦

In her theatrical renunciation of love, Emma Bovary adopts at the corners of her mouth "that immobile contraction that puckers the faces of old maids, and those of men whose ambition has failed," Flaubert writes.

She is pale, and "the skin of her nose was drawn at the nostrils, her eyes had a vague look. After discovering three grey hairs on her temples, she talked much of her old age." We can make out in these behaviors another performance, another show.

She occasionally even faints, *la belle Emma*. But fainting, recall, was part of female speech in that epoch. It was a self-wounding and melodramatic way of expressing one's dissent. One day Emma actually begins to spit blood, to the great distress of her husband, who shuts himself in his study and "wept there, both his elbows on the table."

Like many of Charles Bovary's other gestures, this too could seem extremely ridiculous. But it doesn't make us laugh, since we feel here that the author respects the deep and genuine feeling of his character. Charles may be coarse, wretched, foolish, and unbearable, but the sincerity of his affections is never called into question.

To have help in nursing his wife, Dr. Bovary sends for his mother. But she is hostile to Emma, as much out of jealousy as out of a perfectly justifiable mistrust of a daughter-in-law who is so unstable and so full of herself. Mother Bovary's diagnosis: too many romance novels—they are ruining Emma's mood and her rest. So it is decided, by husband and mother-in-law, that henceforth the only books which may rest in Emma's hands are prayer books.

Emma passively submits, sinking ever deeper into her meekly obedient role. At this point, she no longer even leaves the house. She spends her days in the bedroom, wrapped in one of her silk dressing gowns, watching from her window the people passing by in the street.

It is through that very window one day that she receives the news. One morning she sees a handsome young man dressed in green velvet walking down the street. There is something resolute and magnificent about him that arrests the reclusive young woman's attention.

He is Rodolphe Boulanger, a young manorial lord who lives alone on an estate outside of Yonville. Rodolphe is coming to see Dr. Bovary to have a sick servant of his bled.

This handsome young man must be heading directly for her house, Emma deduces. All of her ennui seems to evaporate in a split second. Contrary to her usual practice, Emma goes downstairs to the study to help her husband with the procedure, and she devotes herself to assisting him as a good nurse would.

Rodolphe, who has a sharp eye for feminine charms, immediately notices her fine white arms. Louise Colet too had famously beautiful white arms; Flaubert praises them in several letters, and certain of Louis Bouilhet's verses echo those praises.

The young lord, revealing himself to be a virtually scientific observer, fixes on all of the details of Emma's body: nice teeth, black eyes, dainty foot, "Parisian" airs. "'She is nice, very nice, that doctor's wife,' he said to himself, '. . . Where did that boor ever pick her up?'"

Rodolphe is thirty-four years old, of brutal temperament and shrewd intelligence. We can see from his behavior that he is used to having his way with women. Sure of himself, decisive and vain, he does not believe that a courtship need last beyond a certain point without having achieved concrete results.

As he observes Emma, in fact, he makes a few precise analyses: "'She must be tired of him, no doubt,'" he thinks, "'He has dirty nails, and hasn't shaven for three days. While he is trotting after his patients, she sits there mending socks. How bored she gets! Poor little woman! She is gaping after love like a carp on the kitchen table after water. Three gallant words and she'd adore me, I'm sure of it. She'd be tender, charming. Yes; but how get rid of her afterwards?'"

Rodolphe already has a lover, an actress, but as soon as he compares her to the naive freshness of Emma, he immediately feels he's had his fill of her. "'Oh, I will have her,'" he says of Emma, "'And that pale complexion! And I, who love pale women!'"

The brutal ways of the young lord are contrasted with his genteel attire. He wears a "batiste shirt with pleated cuffs [that] revealed a waistcoat of grey linen, and his broad-striped trousers disclosed at the ankle nankeen boots with patent leather gaiters. They were so polished that they reflected the grass."

Rodolphe quickly finds a means to be in Emma's company and even to be alone with her. He suggests to her husband that, to divert the poor pallid and sickly woman a bit, he let her ride into the countryside with him.

Dr. Bovary not only consents, he insists that the reluctant Emma accept the young lord's invitation. And she, as if against her will, buys herself a riding habit for the occasion.

It is October, and Emma and Rodolphe leave together on horseback for the woods of Yonville. "Hazy clouds hovered on the horizon between the outlines of the hills." Yonville recedes into the distance behind them. Emma is wearing a man's hat (a detail that again touches on the theme of androgyny) dressed with a blue veil. "Her face appeared in a bluish transparency as if she were floating under azure waves."

The color blue and the odd article of masculine clothing usually have some erotic significance for Flaubert; in his novel *Salammbô*, the beautiful regions, places of desire, are also "mysterious and azured." Salammbô herself will wear the great magic veil of the goddess Tanit that is itself blue. Tanit is also an armed goddess.

Flaubert's cleverness here consists in his way of infecting us with his tastes, which become our own as a result of his style. The reader finds Emma particularly attractive precisely because she wears that man's hat and because her face is partially hidden by a blue veil that mimics the gently sensual effect of swaying ocean waves.

In contrast to Léon, Rodolphe wastes no time in grabbing Emma—so rapidly, in fact, that she becomes frightened and pulls away. He immediately understands that a more graceful approach and more persuasive words will be required. "'In my soul you are as a Madonna on a pedestal,'" he whispers in her ear, "'in a place lofty, secure, immaculate. But I cannot live without you! . . . Be my friend, my sister, my angel!'"

Anyone else could have realized how false these words are. But Emma, who had been fed for so long on speeches just like this, is incapable of recognizing their falseness. Suddenly, it is as if she has fallen inside one of her romance novels, where maudlin youths and haughty heroes freely use such speech. Now she cannot but accept Rodolphe. The way to her heart, above all, is through language.

Rodolphe hooks his arm around her waist. She tries, however feebly, to shake free. He becomes more persistent. She murmurs, "'I shouldn't, I shouldn't! . . . I am out of my mind listening to you!'" Here we are fully immersed in the dialogue of the sentimental romance. A virtuous woman could not but respond in this manner. And when he desperately and bitterly cries "'Why? . . . Emma! Emma!'" she can only murmur, "'Oh, Rodolphe!'" as she leans her forehead against his shoulder.

"She threw back her white neck which swelled in a sigh, and, faltering, weeping, and hiding her face in her hands, with one long shudder, she abandoned herself to him."

The silence of the woods envelops the two impassioned bodies. "Something sweet seemed to come forth from the trees. She felt her heartbeat return, and the blood coursing through her flesh like a river of milk."

This is a rare lyrical moment in a novel so cruel and hard. It is a rare moment in which the characters are left to their pleasures, free of the meddling author's satirical and moralizing voice, always commenting, dissecting, analyzing.

The two lovers return to Yonville, trotting side by side. "She was charming on horseback—upright, with her slender waist, her knee bent on the mane of her horse, her face somewhat flushed by the fresh air in the red of the evening."

In this moment of contemplation, with no hint of moralism or irony, there seems truly to be a cease-fire between the author and his character. Isn't beauty part and parcel of Flaubert's "religion"? How many times in the letters does he speak of beauty, to be enjoyed with a tranquil spirit, as the sole font of all that is good!

"Even now, what I love above all else, is form," Flaubert writes on August 8, 1846, "provided it be beautiful, and nothing beyond it. Women, whose hearts are too ardent and whose minds too exclusive, do not understand this religion of beauty, beauty without feeling. They always demand a cause, an end. I admire tinsel as much as gold: indeed, the poetry of tinsel is even greater, because it is sadder. The only things that exist for me in the world are beautiful verse, well-turned, harmonious, singing sentences, beautiful sunsets, moonlight, pictures, ancient marbles, and strongly marked faces. Beyond that, nothing."

But the contemplation of Emma's beauty does not last long. The moralist champs at the bit. We will see him take off in the scene that immediately follows.

✦❦✦

Charles Bovary meets his wife on her return and is happy to again see her blooming and content. She does not even deign to cast her glance on him, of course. Rather, after liberating herself from his presence, she goes up to her room, locks the door, and walks over to the mirror, in which she gazes at herself for a long time.

"Never had her eyes been so large, so black, nor so deep. Something subtle about her being transfigured her. She repeated: 'I have a lover! a lover!'" She was thrilled by this idea "as if a second puberty had come to her."

We find ourselves again in the slippery realm of Emma's foolish dreams and performances. "She was entering upon a marvelous world where all would be passion, ecstasy, delirium. . . . A blue space surrounded her and ordinary existence appeared only intermittently between these heights, dark and far away beneath her."

The seductive effect of combining the color blue with masculine clothing probably derives from an implicit contradiction between, on one hand, the blue of the sky—that place which inspires pure sentiments and fixed images (gods, icons, statues in plaster or in marble)—and, on the other, the eccentric, the disguised, the perversity of a glimpse between the folds of a woman's garment.

In Emma's head, as we could have predicted, are crowded the rhetorical figures of literary love: a "lyric legion of . . . adulterous women began to sing in her memory with the voice of sisters that charmed her. . . . At long last, as she saw herself among those lovers she had so envied, she fulfilled the love-dream of her youth."

But Emma's is not merely a disinterested enthusiasm, however saturated it may be by the bad books she has read. "A satisfaction of revenge" also echoes in her, as Flaubert allows us to perceive. "How she had suffered! But she had won out at last."

From that afternoon on, Emma and Rodolphe take up writing to each other regularly every day. Gustave and Louise had done exactly the same thing. She had asked for, virtually demanded, a letter a day, and he had told her that it was that injunction itself that prevented him from writing her that often. He finally gave in; but then, he loved to write letters, and he started sending her long missives almost daily.

57

In the novel, Emma leaves her letters in the back end of the garden, in a crack of the little terrace wall. Rodolphe comes to retrieve them and substitutes one of his own; Emma constantly complains of their brevity. Louise too had complained of how short Flaubert's letters were after the first months, during which he had flooded her with paper.

The great actress has switched parts, Flaubert suggests. Now Emma sets about performing, with grave determination and skill, the role of the adulteress that she recognized in the mirror and welcomed with such vindictive joy.

One night, she slips into bed with her husband and pretends to fall asleep. When she is sure that he is asleep, she gets out of bed "holding her breath, smiling, half undressed," and goes to meet her lover at the end of the garden. Rodolphe wraps her in his large black cloak, pressing her tightly to himself. He often is unable to suppress some vulgar allusion to her husband, who sleeps a short distance away.

This is perhaps the first time in the entire novel that we find Emma in the grip of delicate feelings. Even despite Flaubert's surly severity, he seems to acknowledge in this woman, taxed with every possible flaw, a gleam not necessarily of affection, nor of tenderness, nor loyalty, but of a kind of conjugal solidarity.

Rodolphe's facetiousness seems truly to bother her. Why ridicule poor Charles, whose generosity is so complete that not a single doubt or suspicion has ever crossed his mind?

But Flaubert, as usual, is hovering in the background, pipe between his teeth, shaking his head. Don't delude yourselves, readers: that conjugal solidarity will transform itself in the blink of an eye according to the logic of characterization. Emma is not concerned for her husband but, rather, for a certain lack of pathos in that moment. "She would have liked to see him more serious, and even on occasions more dramatic." Less an offense to the person of Charles, Rodolphe's behavior is an offense to the clichés of literary adultery.

The same scene repeats itself two days later. When Emma believes she hears footsteps in the garden, she asks Rodolphe if he has brought his pistols. When he asks her why, and she says "'to defend yourself,'" he chuckles, "'From your husband? Oh, the poor fellow,'" accompanying the remark with a gesture that signifies: "'I could crush him with a flip of my finger.'"

Emma seems torn between her admiration for the "bravery" of her lover and her dislike of "a sort of indecency" in him, "and a naive coarseness that scandalised her."

Nevertheless, Rodolphe's lack of delicacy does not prevent Emma from continuing to become more indiscreet and more sentimental. Early one morning, she is taken with a sudden desire to rush to see her lover. With absolutely no concern for the danger of being seen, she hurries to his side through the muddy fields so she can embrace him upon his waking.

She also insists "on exchanging miniatures," exactly the way Louise did. She places a dark lock of hair in the one she gives him. "And now she was asking for a ring—a real wedding-ring, in token of eternal union," as she tells him. Shortly thereafter, she asks him about his mother—who, it turns out, has been dead for twenty years, as Flaubert wryly puts it. But Emma, relentless, dedicates verses to him as if he were a recently orphaned child. Gazing at the moon, she whispers to him, "'I am sure that, from up there, both [mothers] approve our love.'"

Emma's passion, in all its goofy and patently absurd aspects, is turned inside out like a sock. Blind as a bat, she understands absolutely nothing of the coarseness of Rodolphe's character and presses him with stock romantic gestures, little blandishments in the manner of the heroines of serial novels. Could anything be more unwarranted? Flaubert seems to say.

Indeed, after a series of episodes taken from the manual of perfect adultery, Rodolphe plainly begins to get bored. But how to get her out of his hair? And yet, something still remains which continues to make him feel bound to her. "But she was so pretty! He had possessed so few women of similar ingenuousness."[4]

Louise too was "pretty" and had pale skin, as Flaubert constantly repeats in his letters. And he was certainly attracted to her,

4. This is de Man's accurate translation of Flaubert's "Il en avait possédé si peu d'une candeur pareille." The Italian translation of Madame Bovary that Maraini employs, however, renders this as "aveva la pelle di un candore che non aveva mai visto"—literally, "she had skin of a pale hue that he had never seen before." Apparently, the Italian translator confused the word peu with peau, which means "skin" in French. Maraini's subsequent reference to Louise's pale skin is based on this mistranslation.

as Rodolphe was to Emma, notwithstanding the annoyance her mannerisms provoked in him.

"You want me to come crawling at your knees as if I were fifteen years old, want me to fly to you, to tremble, to cry even; you promise to leave me a memory of you as if it were some kind of vengeance," Gustave wrote to Louise on January 21, 1847, only a year after they had begun seeing each other. And on November 7 of the same year, he wrote: "I love your face, and everything about you is sweet. But, but—I am so weary! So bored, so fundamentally incapable of making anyone happy! Make you happy! Ah, poor Louise, *I* make a woman *happy!* I don't even know how to play with a child. My mother snatches away her little granddaughter when I touch her, for I make her cry, and she is like you, always calling me and wanting to be near me."

"This love without debauchery," Flaubert explains to us about Rodolphe, "was a new experience for him, and, drawing him out of his lazy habits, caressed at once his pride and his sensuality."

"Although his bourgeois common sense disapproved of it, Emma's exaltations, deep down in his heart, enchanted him, since they were directed his way. Then, sure of her love, he no longer made an effort, and insensibly his manner changed."

Emma Bovary reacts, as usual, inappropriately. Not able to understand the man she loves, she decides to conquer him again with sentimentalisms and laments. Louise had done the same thing, alternating complaint and effusive affection in response to Gustave's rude and cold manners.

"The humiliation of having given in turned into resentment, tempered by their voluptuous pleasures. It was not tenderness; it was like a continual seduction. He held her fully in his power; she almost feared him."

The oft-noted dynamic that destroys all self-respect! First delight and then humiliation, rancor, and the chill of a pleasure reduced to pure sexual egotism. Trust, tenderness, and generosity are gone, while only the single-minded pursuit of physical enjoyment and a desire for power remain.

They keep each other continually within view, each watching for the other's next false step. Can you see now, Flaubert seems to be asking, how quickly a love devoid of friendship can transform itself into abuse and fear, lust and torpor?

One day Emma receives a letter from her aged father, the kind Théodore Rouault, who loves her and worries about her, even though from afar. Memories of the time when she lived with him on the farm occur spontaneously to her. "What happiness she had known at that time. . . . What a wealth of illusions!" are the thoughts Flaubert puts in her mind. But what is it that makes her so unhappy now? Where is the "extraordinary catastrophe [that] had destroyed her life"?

That evening, during her meeting with Rodolphe, Emma appears cold, distant. To gain revenge, he punishes her by missing the next three meetings. At this point, Emma begins to think it has all been a mistake. Why did she not know how to love her husband? she asks herself in a rare moment of sincerity; Why hadn't she been faithful to him? What would you bet, Flaubert smirkingly implies, that she will soon gravitate toward a new notion, be moved by a newly theatrical "sacrificial intention"?

The occasion arises as a result of an event involving her husband the doctor. Homais, the town pharmacist, proposes that Dr. Bovary operate on the clubfoot of Hippolyte, the stable boy at the Lion d'Or, Yonville's inn. If Charles cures him, through what would certainly be a simple procedure, all of the newspapers will report it. He will become famous, and the pharmacist as well. Homais will assist the doctor in the operation, and the two of them cannot but be congratulated and lauded throughout the land.

Could it be accidental that the victim is named Hippolyte, just like Louise Colet's husband? Is not the ever-afflicted stable boy the symbol of her husband's sacrifice upon the altar of Louise's worldly and literary ambitions?

Emma seriously considers supporting Charles in his project. If it is a success, her reputation will rise with his, as will her material fortune (a not unpleasant prospect). "She only longed to lean on something more solid than love," a thing which at that moment seems only treacherous and threatening.

As we know, the operation fails miserably. Hippolyte nearly dies of gangrene, gripped by horrendous pain. Another more expert, and truly famous, doctor comes to Yonville to amputate the poor stable boy's leg. Charles Bovary comes out of this experience mortified and defeated. Emma, in her ambitious egotism, refuses to forgive him for it, conveniently forgetting that she had decided to be among the project's supporters.

"Emma . . . watched him; she did not share his humiliation; she felt another—that of having imagined that such a man could have any worth, as if twenty times already she had not sufficiently perceived his mediocrity."

By now, everything about her husband irritated her: his way of talking, his way of dressing, his face, his hands, his entire body. "She repented of her past virtue as of a crime, and what still remained of it crumbled away beneath the furious blows of her pride."

Do we think that, had the operation been a tremendous professional success for Dr. Bovary, Emma would have given up her adultery? Maybe, Flaubert tells us, but not for reasons of integrity. Only the doctor's newfound fame, and that halo of public esteem that would have surrounded him, could have sufficiently flattered Emma's vanity to provide her with another move in her game: playing the wife of a man respected in his profession, with good social connections, money, and leisure. This new role, however, would still have been a sham.

Once the enterprise has failed, Emma is unable to feel any sympathy for the man who tried, without any self-aggrandizing intentions, out of pure altruism and weakness in the face of the stupid ambitions of Homais, to perform this surgical experiment. Charles knows no ambitions; it would be accurate for him to say, as Flaubert says of himself in a letter to Louise, "I've dug out my own hole and I live in it, careful to keep the temperature inside the same" (August 26, 1846).

But Emma is incapable of discrimination. Only the concrete and visible matter to her. And when these are lacking, understanding even the most simple of things is impossible for her. She proves to be pitiless, vicious, with her husband. "She revelled in all the evil ironies of triumphant adultery. The memory of her lover came back to her with irresistible, dizzying attractions; she threw her whole soul towards this image, carried by renewed passion."

Charles, in a moment of despair, comes to her seeking some consolation. But she turns on him like a viper: "'Don't touch me!'" she cries, "flushed with anger." "'What is it? what is it?'" he asks, bewildered and wounded. "'You know that I love you,'" he meekly and uncomprehendingly insists. "'Stop it!'" she shrieks "with a terrible look." And she rushes out, slamming the door. Charles falls into an armchair, wondering why his wife had been so angry. Is it some nervous illness? Too dim, he is unable to understand, cannot guess, what is going on in his wife's mind and is unable to imagine how full of discontent and mortified desire she is. But if he did understand her motivations, it would mean having to let Emma go, and this Charles cannot do. Feeling that their relationship is out of his control, he humbly, blindly, out of neither calculation nor cowardliness, prefers to let things take their course, placing all his hopes on the presumed solidity of a marriage for love, not money. And yet the cruel voice of Emma resounds in his ears, making him feel that "something fatal and incomprehensible was whirling around him."

When Rodolphe appears that evening in the rear of the garden, "he found his mistress waiting for him. . . . They threw their arms round one another, and all their rancor melted like snow beneath the warmth of that kiss."

Emma by now has decided: she will run away with Rodolphe. That husband of hers does not deserve her; their marriage humiliates and suffocates her. She discusses her decision with Rodolphe, who seems by no means thrilled with the idea but who, for the moment, is willing to make the best of a worsening situation. From this point on, Emma considers herself to be a stranger in her own home. She spends her time filing her nails, polishing them with lemon, covering her body with cold cream, and perfuming her handkerchiefs and blouses with patchouli. "She loaded herself with bracelets, rings, and necklaces . . . and prepared herself and her room like a courtesan receiving a prince."

Furthermore, she continues to go into debt at an increasing pace, buying costly gifts for her lover on credit from the merchant Lheureux: for a silver-handled riding crop alone she spends more than 270 francs, Flaubert meticulously explains. And then come the suede gloves, the silver cigar case, the famous medallion, and so on.

It is by no means accidental that while writing his novel, Flaubert decided not to let Louise Colet read a single line of it. Having made up with her after three and a half years of silence, he had begun to flirt with her again. Too many things could have offended her, too many coincidences, too many similarities.

And yet Flaubert was in the habit of showing his writings to Louise. Had she not been one of the first to read *The Temptation of Saint Anthony*, even before the book's publication was being considered? She had even read the first draft, from 1843, of *Sentimental Education*. Furthermore, she had always had intelligent and complimentary things to say about his work.

It should be noted, of course, that Flaubert normally loved to read his work to as many people as possible. His invitations to readings at Croisset have become legendary; such events lasted from five to six hours and ended in the middle of the night, leaving everyone exhausted.

"At four o'clock we were at Flaubert's . . . to hear a reading of *Salammbô*," write the Goncourt brothers in their diary of May 6, 1861. "From four until seven Flaubert read aloud in his moving, sonorous voice that cradles you in a sound like a bronze murmur. At seven we dined, [. . .] and directly after dinner, with time out for a single pipe, the reading was resumed; and between readings and summary accounts of certain sections of the book (some of them not completely finished), [. . .] it was two in the morning before he got through the last chapter."[5]

The Goncourts are credited with originally reporting Flaubert's obsession with the works of de Sade. "He is incredible, this de Sade, everywhere you look you find him in Flaubert, like a

5. *The Goncourt Journals*, ed. and trans. Galantière, 10. My interpolated ellipses indicate places where Galantière omitted sentences from the original passage without providing ellipses of his own. My first ellipsis marks the excision of a paragraph on Pradier, the sculptor. The paragraph following that begins with "And directly after dinner" (*"Puis après le dîner"*). My second ellipsis roughly substitutes for the phrase *"la baisade de Salammbô et de Mathô."* A less chaste and more complete translation of the Goncourts' meaning here might be "the reading recommences, with readings and summary accounts of certain sections of the book, right to the end of the last completed chapter, Salammbô and Mathô's screw. It is two o'clock in the morning, and we are still there." Cf. Edmond and Jules de Goncourt, *Journal: Mémoires de la vie littéraire* (Monaco: Fasquelle and Flammarion, 1956), 4:189. Maraini's version loses none of these subtleties.

horizon" (April 10, 1860).[6] "Flaubert visits. He is truly fixated on de Sade. . . . He makes him into the incarnation of Antiphysis, and he goes so far as to say, in one of his best paradoxes, that he is the logical conclusion of catholicism, the loathing of the body" (April 9, 1861). "Spent the evening at Flaubert's. Bouilhet, who has the look of a real working man, was there. Amazing legends of provincial avarice. . . . Then, chat about Sade, to whom Flaubert's mind, as if fascinated, always returns" (January 29, 1860).[7]

It was also the Goncourt brothers who first related the phenomena of Flaubert's life as a writer that today we would call psychosomatic: "Gustave told us that when he was writing the scene of Madame Bovary's poisoning, he felt as if he had a huge brass plate lying on his stomach, a sensation which made him vomit twice" (December 10, 1860).

"Flaubert told us that when he was a child he would so lose himself in books, nibbling his tongue and twisting his hair with his fingers, that he would occasionally fall out of his chair on to the floor. One day he cut his nose, falling against a bookcase" (January 11, 1863).[8]

"Flaubert, sitting Turkish fashion on his divan, talking of his plans, his ambitions, his dreams, confiding in us his great and continued desire to write a novel about the modern Orient. . . . We all moved into the sitting room, and there Flaubert was asked to dance 'The Drawing-room Idiot.' He borrowed a tail coat from Gautier, raised his collar, and of his hair, his face, his whole physiognomy he made something, I hardly know what, which transformed him suddenly into a fantastic caricature of a cretin" (March 29, 1862).[9]

Flaubert himself writes: "This book, at this point in the writing of it, tortures me so much (and if I could find another word to express it I would use it) that I often get physically ill. It has been three weeks that I have been virtually fainting from the pain. At

6. "*C'est étonnant, ce de Sade, on le trouve à tous les bouts de Flaubert comme un horizon*" (de Goncourt, *Journal*, 3:248).
7. Galantière paraphrases this passage as: "Spent the evening at Flaubert's with Bouilhet talking about de Sade[,] to whom Flaubert, as if fascinated, constantly reverts" (*The Goncourt Journals*, ed. and trans. Galantière, 83).
8. Ibid., 138.
9. Ibid., 117–18.

other moments I feel suffocated or feel the impulse to vomit at the dinner table" (October 17, 1853).

The life Flaubert shared with his friends was made up of meetings, dinners, evening readings, but also of writing together and, with those with whom he was more intimate, editing each other.

Before being replaced by Bouilhet, Maxime Du Camp, among the more assiduous of Flaubert's friends in Croisset, spent entire nights discussing and correcting with his steel pen (Flaubert still used goose quill) his friend's manuscripts.

And Louis Bouilhet, some years later, wrote: "I will come to Croisset on Thursday, and dedicate myself completely to your novel. We will go over all of the first part, word by word" (January 19, 1866).

"I read the last twenty pages [of *Madame Bovary*] to Bouilhet who is pleased with them," Flaubert wrote to Louise on July 26, 1852; "Next Sunday I plan to reread all of it to him. . . . To you, however, I won't read anything. I will be coy with you and won't show you even a single line, however much I want to do the opposite. But this makes more sense; you will be better able to judge, and you will enjoy it more, if it is well done. Another long year yet."

But clearly Flaubert's decision has less to do with coyness than with prudence. This relationship between Flaubert and Louise Colet, which starts up again after almost four years of silence and separate lives, is truly curious.

The correspondence from the first period of their attachment is passionate and contradictory. Naturally, we can only speak of his letters to her, since hers have been lost, destroyed perhaps by Flaubert himself, who was bashful and jealously guarded his feelings and those he elicited in others. Having been disturbed by the publication of Mérimée's uncollected letters, Gustave and Louis Bouilhet decided to burn all the letters they had exchanged as young boys. Maxime does likewise. As a result, Flaubert's correspondence with his two closest friends today exists in damaged form.

As far as Louise Colet's carefully preserved correspondence with Flaubert from their second period is concerned, we find its tone to be one much more of master and student rather than of lover and beloved. She sends him her writings, always prolix, always teeming with her literary enthusiasms, always awkward and labored, traits he calls to her attention with a frankness at times decidedly sadistic. Sartre notes in *The Family Idiot* that Flaubert's masochism was obvious, but no less so than his sadism, which was born of his negative pride and of his rancorous and exasperated dreams.

"I won't make any comments to you about the second part of *Fantômes* because there is almost nothing about it that I like," Flaubert writes to Louise on September 1, 1852. "Do you know what you lack the most? Discernment. One cannot acquire it by sponging one's head with cold water, dear savage. You do and you write whatever crosses your mind without worrying about how it will end. . . . Use your eyes for seeing and not for crying. . . . You so link your concepts and your passions that you weaken the first and prevent yourself from fully experiencing the second. . . . Oh, if I could make you into what it is I dream of, what a woman you would be!"

Elsewhere, he writes: "You declaim, you don't write. . . . No, no, no, I cannot accept this rubbish." "What infuriates me . . . is your hard-headedness, . . . your brain is day-by-day becoming an object of my amazement, it almost dizzies me. . . . In this comedy [that you sent me] there are some admirable things[,] . . . some excellent verses, . . . side by side with inconceivable weaknesses, emptiness, and redundancy. . . . It is both very good and very bad at the same time."

"To make literature as a woman, you must first have passed over the waters of the Styx" (December 23, 1853). "There are two strands in you, my Muse, one a dramatic sense, made up not of theatrical gestures but of expressions, which is superior, and the other an instinctive understanding of color, of contrast. These two qualities have been and still are shot through with two flaws, one of which you possess by character, and the other by sex: the first is philosophism, the maxim, political, social, democratic speechifying, all of that nonsense which comes from Voltaire, and from which old Victor Hugo is by no means exempt. The second weakness is of vagueness, the female obsession with tenderness. There is no need, when one has reached your level, for the sheets to smell of milk" (April 13, 1853).

And yet, even in this second phase of their correspondence, moments of tenderness are not completely lacking. There is the memory, however faintly cloying, of past love: "I have never loved you so much. I had an ocean of cream in my soul" (June 9, 1852). There is the sweetness of freely conversing with a friend: "How much I enjoy talking to you; I let my pen go on without even realizing how late it is; it lets me flow, this conveying all my thoughts to you as they occur, to you, the best thoughts of my heart." There is the pleasure of openly sharing the most homey and familiar things: "For the last twenty-five years my mother has had a maid she believed to be very dedicated. She has found out instead that the woman was 'abusing her privileges,' as the phrase goes, and in addition to everything else was almost entirely feeding a brother (a buffoon, not in the least funny, of the most stupid and base kind) at our expense." There is the satisfaction of speaking of his own work as if to himself: "*Bovary* is still dragging, but making a little bit of progress. . . . I have reread quite a bit of it. The style is uneven and too methodical. You can feel the nails gripping the planks of the hull too tightly. I need to leave more play. But how? What a rotten profession!" (March 25, 1853). There is his habit of scolding her: "You are jealous of the sand that my feet have touched, even though not a single grain of it ever entered my skin, while I carry in my heart the huge gash that you left there?" And there is the vanity of his speaking to her with the tone of a connoisseur of women: "As far as Kuchuk-Hânem is concerned, set your mind to rest and at the same time revise your ideas of the Orient. Be assured that she felt nothing. . . . She thought of us as great noble cawadja (gentlemen) because we left her no small amount of coins, that's all. . . . The oriental woman is a machine, nothing more; she makes no distinction between one man and another. Smoking, going to the baths, painting her eyelids, and drinking coffee, this is the circle of occupations within which her whole existence revolves. As far as physical pleasure is concerned, it must be quite faint in them, given that they have the famous button cut off at a very early age. . . . This is what makes them so poetic from a certain point of view, that they return fully to nature. . . . From whence derives this majesty of their forms? Perhaps from the absence of all passion. They have the beauty of ruminating bulls, of running greyhounds, of gliding eagles. The fatalism which fills them, their belief in the nothingness which is human existence, imparts to their movements, their poses, their expressions, an air of grandeur and resignation[,] . . . and then the sun, the sun. And an immense ennui which devours everything. When I write oriental poetry (because I too will write some, since it is in fashion and everyone is writing it), it is this that I will try to bring out. . . . You say Kuchuk-Hânem's lice debase her in your eyes; in mine they make her even more enchanting. Their nauseating odor mingles with the scent of her skin dripping with sandalwood" (March 27, 1853).

Emma and Rodolphe's relationship has become a one-way conversation. "'Do you love me?'" she asks. "'Why, of course I love you,'" he vaguely responds. "'A great deal?'" she persists, "'You haven't loved any others?'" "'Did you think you'd got a virgin?'" he crudely replies. "'I love you so . . . ,'" she continues in a monotone, "'I am your servant, your concubine! You are my king, my idol! You are good, you are beautiful, you are clever, you are strong!'"

In this scene, we seem to be rereading Gustave's words to Louise: "You think of me a little as Madame de Sévigné thought of Louis XIV: 'Oh, what a great king!' because he had danced with her. Because you love me you think me handsome, intelligent, sublime; you predict great things for me. No! No! You are mistaken" (October 7, 1846).

But Rodolphe is not Flaubert. In fact, while Louise's letters "irritate" the young Gustave and make him want to keep his distance from his passionate literary lover, Emma's declarations to the young lord elicit other judgments, more trivial and facile, from him: "He had so often heard these things said that they didn't strike him as original. Emma was like all his mistresses; and the charm of novelty, gradually falling away like a garment, laid bare the eternal monotony of passion."

And, "with the superiority of critical insight of the person who holds back his emotions in any engagement, Rodolphe perceived that there were other pleasures to be exploited in this love. He discarded all modesty as inconvenient. He treated her without consideration. And he made her into something at once malleable and corrupt."

And what does Emma do? How does she react to this metamorphosis in their love? Neither with anguish nor with revenge, as one might think. Flaubert seems to perfectly understand the workings of self-deprecation, almost as if he had studied them within himself. The foot slips on adulation, and as a result we fall into an idol worship of the beloved one who demeans us.

Emma, in fact, acquiesces. And not only that, she even goes so far as to change her way of walking and behaving: "Her glances were bolder, her speech freer." Here Flaubert unintentionally clarifies an idea that all patriarchal societies have always had, that the emancipation of daughters begins with their discovery and exploration of sexual pleasure.

"She even went as far as to go out walking with Rodolphe, a cigarette in her mouth, 'just to scandalize the town.'" Sometime after that escapade, the people of Yonville see her getting out of a post chaise "wearing a tight-fitting waistcoat cut like a man's."

Once again, Flaubert brings us back to the theme of androgyny, but without ever ultimately forcing open the door to the abyss. If going about in a man's waistcoat with a cigarette dangling from one's lips means bearing the signs of a transgression of gender roles, we are still, Flaubert seems to tell us, only in the realm of mere trickery. This elaborate game of switching genders ends with the gratuitous assertion of an empty gesture.

In the meanwhile, Emma's mother-in-law arrives at the home of Dr. Bovary and is scandalized to find her daughter-in-law in such a state of extravagant neglectfulness, devoid of interest in her house, her daughter, her husband.

She accuses her, as usual, of reading too many novels. And she accuses her son of not having known how to prevent his wife's so willful misuse of literature.

But this time Emma refuses to stand for it, paying her outraged mother-in-law back in kind for her criticism. Clearly, this insubordination is regarded by Flaubert as a result of Emma's "corruption." The two women begin to argue viciously, while poor Charles, beside himself, wonders what he can possibly do to bring peace back to his family. He is very attached to his mother, but certainly he loves his wife more. He would like to defend the one without wounding the other. But how to manage it?

Emma now more than ever places all her hopes on escape. "She leant on [Rodolphe's] shoulder murmuring: 'Think, we will soon be in the mail-coach! Can you imagine?'" He doesn't refuse but seems, rather, to encourage the plan. A moment of reflection, however, would have sufficed to convince him that he has absolutely no desire to put it into action. But, on Emma's insistence, they finally set a date.

"Never had Madame Bovary been so beautiful as at this period," the author comments. We think: perhaps this time he will grant a bit of leniency to the poor, unfortunate Emma, lost in her dream of love but ready, for once, to make a concrete and real decision in her life. "She had that indefinable beauty that results from joy, from enthusiasm, from success. . . . Her half-closed eyelids seemed perfectly shaped for the long languid glances that escaped from them; her breathing dilated the fine nostrils and raised the fleshy corners of her mouth."

"Some artist skilled in corruption seemed to have devised the shape of her hair as it fell on her neck, coiled in a heavy mass, casually reassembled after being loosened daily in adultery."

In the bed of her husband, Emma envisions her flight, her ecstatic renunciation, her inaccessibility. But even in these fantasies—and here, again, we see Flaubert smirking—our heroine appears incorrigibly affected and common. "They would live in a low, flat-roofed house, shaded by a palm-tree, in the heart of a gulf, by the sea. They would row in gondolas, swing in hammocks, and their existence would be easy and free as their wide silk gowns, warm and star-spangled as the night they would contemplate."

We learn from Flaubert's letters that Louise Colet often dreamed of departing for Venice, where she had stayed as a child with her father, and that she dreamed of gondolas and palm trees, often confusing Venice with Cairo. But Louise was far too poor to be able to afford such a voyage. Nor was Gustave ever generous enough to invite her along on one of his extended pilgrimages, as he did instead with his friend Maxime Du Camp or with Louis Bouilhet.

But no matter how conventional Louise's dreams were, they probably never attained the level of poor taste that Flaubert attributes to the Emma of his novel. Flaubert himself spent entire days concocting imaginary voyages to Italy, Africa, and the Far East. His fantasies of world travel were at times not all that dissimilar from the silly dreams Emma and Louise entertained. Like the popular culture of his day, he too was possessed by a shimmering, compensatory fascination with the exotic, and he was well aware of it.

The day set for Emma's departure at last arrives. But Rodolphe finds an excuse: he asks her for a fifteen-day postponement. Emma, not suspecting anything, agrees. What else could she have done? Her plan is so vague that it takes no idea either of their destination or their means of economic support, or anything else, into account. She entrusts all of the details of the plan to her lover. The only thing she herself does is order a traveling cloak and bag from her friend Lheureux.

Finally, after Rodolphe requests two more delays, the definitive date of departure is set: Monday, September 4. The night before they are to set out, the two lovers meet in the woods outside of Yonville to make last-minute arrangements. Rodolphe seems sad to Emma, and she asks him why—but he doesn't answer. "'Do you love me? Swear it then!'" she urges him. "'Do I love you? Do I? But I adore you, my love!'" he replies, trying to sound convincing. But it is clear that he has other things on his mind.

"'Till to-morrow then!'" Emma says, full of faith. He nods his assent. She makes her way home. He turns to watch her go, and "when he saw her with her white gown gradually fade away in the shade like a ghost, his heart beat so wildly that he had to support himself against a tree."

His thought process at this point, however, becomes very practical: "'What a fool I am!' he said, swearing a dreadful oath. 'All the same, she was the prettiest mistress ever. . . . For, after all, . . . I can't exile myself, and with a child on my hands to boot! . . . And beside, the worries, the cost! No, no, a thousand times no! It would have been too stupid.'"

The next morning, Emma receives a letter hidden in a basket of apricots. "*Du courage, Emma, du courage!*" writes the hypocrite Rodolphe, "I don't want to be the one to ruin your life . . . "

While Emma is reading the fatal letter, Flaubert returns to Rodolphe—with extraordinary narrative effect, much as in a film flashback—to display him commenting to himself on the letter as he writes it: "'Poor little woman! . . . She'll think me harder than a rock. There ought to have been some tears on this.' . . . Then, having emptied some water into a glass, Rodolphe dipped his finger into it, and let a big drop fall on the paper, making a pale stain on the ink."

Emma reads Rodolphe's words, and her first impulse is to throw herself from the window of the attic, where she has hidden to read the letter without being disturbed. But she doesn't do it. She simply faints, exactly as she had done when she learned that she had given birth to a daughter, not a son. Fainting is one way to bring the curtain down on a scene that is too starkly painful.

A short while later, Charles arrives and her daughter runs to embrace her, but Emma repulses them all: "'No, no. . . . I want no one!'" she cries. Then she faints again.

For forty-three days Emma, stricken by brain fever, languishes in a delirium, her weeping husband beside her. Finally, the reader says, here is true human suffering. A woman who has bet everything on a man, on escape, whom we see wretchedly abandoned— doesn't it make sense, isn't it right, that she experience real pain, true discomfort?

And yet, no. Even this moment of suffering is deformed by the grotesque. Emma, Flaubert tells us, finds a way to dramatize the event, to stage it in one of her beloved theaters. But what scene is left for Madame Bovary to play? The mystical crisis! What better occasion than this for her to take on a part that is so unique? Once again we find her, in a plight which seems so agonizing, already intent on studying her new role, that of the martyr expecting sanctification.

As soon as Emma can open her mouth, she sends her husband off to find a priest. When she is then sprinkled with holy water, she "[fancied] she heard in space the music of seraphic harps, and perceived in an azure sky, on a golden throne in the midst of saints holding green palms, God the Father, resplendent with majesty, who ordered to earth angels with wings of fire to carry her away in their arms."

"She wanted to become a saint. She bought rosaries and wore holy medals; she wished to have in her room, by the side of her bed, a reliquary set in emeralds that she might kiss it every evening."

"Madame Bovary's mind was not yet sufficiently clear," Flaubert dryly comments, "to apply herself seriously to anything." Nevertheless, she immerses herself in a variety of devotional texts. "When the volume slipped from her hands, she fancied herself seized with the finest Catholic melancholy ever conceived by an ethereal soul."

In this muddle of notions and sensations we can already see the entire kernel of *Bouvard and Pécuchet*. Emma too, like all great dilettantes, loves to try her hand at various occupations, regardless of how diverse they might be one from another, regardless that each one, with its own enormous body of accompanying knowledge, would take years of study and professional practice to absorb.

But Emma, as we know, is a dabbler, a female Don Quixote viewed with an unsympathetic eye. She cannot stand either discipline or studiousness, our Madame Bovary. She dreams of mastering things she has no knowledge of because she's heard—or, rather, read—about them. Her cool aloofness cannot help but elicit both compassion and annoyance in us.

We could say that Emma was a product of the general condition of all "young ladies of good family" during the nineteenth century—with lots of dreams, lots of fantasies, no real in-depth knowledge of anything, no professionalism, no diligence. Female writers were considered to have no real "training": How could one speak of love when one was still being chaperoned, when every liberty was still considered libertinism?

Ready to faint as a way of saying no, but as a way of saying yes as well, these young women were forced to "savagely" utilize the language of the body, the only kind given them to express.

But Flaubert has no pity for Emma's weaknesses and has no wish to historicize her, as his friend Henry James might have. Nor is he interested in putting the deepest complexities of female discontent under the microscope, as another of his renowned friends by the name of Turgenev did.

Flaubert takes great pleasure in representing Emma's various theatrical incarnations with a self-satisfied meticulousness. However, after relating how Emma casts herself in the role of the "saint," he tells us that even the most thrilling of her performances always come to an end, for the simple reason that Emma bores herself. On the other hand, if she doggedly portrayed the same character, wouldn't she become a sort of specialist in the field, almost an artist?

Underneath Emma's dilettantism there is not a single real feeling, not even of curiosity about the subject matter she pretends to have mastered as if it were her true vocation.

Thus, while at the beginning of her illness her bedroom became the gathering place of pious women friends and priests, as her appetite begins to return so does her intolerance for the very same visitors who had been witnesses to her religious conversion.

The healthier her body becomes, the more her mystical fervor weakens. Her tone of voice becomes sharper, stronger, and her charitable works drop off almost entirely. Homais, the pharmacist, suggests that Charles Bovary "give madame some distraction by taking her to the theatre," which would aid in her convalescence. She is still so pale and thin. But Emma will not hear of it.

Shedding her new character, however boring it has become, is difficult and trying for Emma every time.

Charles insists, sure it "would do her good." And, as always, he is absolutely sincere. We begin to suspect that he is the only character toward whom Flaubert demonstrates a secret, subterranean, and affectionate condescension.

One evening Emma finally agrees, and they both dress to the nines to go to Rouen to see *Lucia di Lammermoor*.

E mma, Flaubert says, loves music—or, to be more precise, loves melodrama. Her tastes, however, do not run toward the essence of music, even in its simplest and most easily enjoyable forms such as arias and popular duets. Instead, her interest lingers on whatever of the sentimental, the hyperbolic, and the folkloristic exist in opera librettos.

During the first act of *Lammermoor* in the theater in Rouen, we see our heroine leaning languidly against the rail of their box, apparently enthralled by the music. Actually, her attention has been captured by the tenor, who seems so handsome and so charming that she dreams of his carrying her off on a stormy night. Sweet, incurable Emma—we do not know whether to defend her from her author or to ignominiously abandon her to her unbearable cartoonishness.

At intermission, Charles goes to the refreshment room to get something to drink. When he returns, he says to his wife: "'Just guess whom I met up there! Monsieur Léon! . . . He's coming along to pay his respects.'"

From that moment on, Emma no longer pays attention to the opera, completely forgetting the singer who had so seduced her a few minutes earlier, and forgetting as well the captivating lyrics to which she had so enthusiastically abandoned herself.

Thinking of Léon, she recalls all the tête-à-têtes by the fire; "all the sadness of their love, so calm and so protracted, so discreet, so tender" returns to her memory.

When the handsome Léon enters their box, she is happy to see him, and when he asks her if the opera does not bore her, she admits it does, it bores her greatly. Thus, over the timid protests of Charles that he, truly, is enjoying the music and paying close attention to it, they decide to leave.

The three take a stroll while sipping on rum sherbets. At this point, Léon suggests that they return the next day to see the act that they've just missed. Dr. Bovary replies that he, unfortunately, must head back to Yonville, but asks his wife if she would "'like to stay by yourself, my darling?'"—happy to make her happy.

Once again, it is he, the loving and concerned husband, who gives his wife the opportunity to betray him. But in Charles there is neither cynicism nor design. Since his love exists above all else, he is genuinely happy to see his wife doing better, amusing herself a little after so much suffering.

One might say that Charles's actions are those of a fool rather than a cynic and that, at this point, it is all his own fault. But a husband who doesn't want to know will never find anything out, not even if the facts are laid out right before his eyes. One might wonder why a husband would not want to find out that his wife has wronged him. Could it be out of fear of confronting the consequences? Or because he wants his own similarly secret misdeeds to be justified? Could it be out of a complete lack of interest in what his wife does? Or of a desire to be left in peace, come what may? Or of a masochistic pleasure in suffering? Or could it be because his sexual response requires exactly that—the sight or the thought of his wife with another? Or because he likes the convenience of having a wife at home, and he knows he can obtain this only by allowing her a measure of sexual freedom? The possible reasons are many, and all plausible.

It seems clear, however, that none of these reasons is sufficient to explain the blindness of Charles Bovary. Let us remember that in school they called him "Charbovari" because of the timidity which caused him to stutter, and that they teased him about his clumsiness and cowardliness. We also remember it was his mother who made him finish his medical degree, since he, on his own, would have lived on dreams and never amounted to anything. We remember that in class, while the other boys carelessly tossed their caps underneath their desks, Charles clutched his so tightly to his chest that the others thought he was a dunce. Let us remember that his mother was the one who found him his first position as a municipal doctor and who married him to a rich widow (who later lost everything and died of a broken heart).

In a certain sense, Charles, like Emma, lives on dreams. But his are simple dreams, having nothing to do with literature. There is no danger he would ever be caught reading a book. He is always on the road, always on his poor mount, but to little positive effect. Charles is the kind who always wastes time, who prefers the tepidness of his tiny imagination to the excessive heat of reality.

It is for this reason, perhaps, that Charles and Emma at bottom make a good couple. They both turn their faces away from the concreteness of the world. Only Emma acts and dreams up a world made of sentimental hyperbole, while Charles holds on to the few certain things in his life: his love for his wife, his tenderness for his daughter, and his affectionate regard for his mother. There is no room left in his heart for anything else. He is like all other people who fix on one or two details of life and tend to enlarge them, adapt them to their own uses, nurture them, and hold them dear.

Charles, who is a big tall bear of a man (Wasn't Flaubert also big and tall? Wasn't he also regarded as something of a dolt, even an idiot, by his family when he was a boy?), is poignantly aware of his bulk, and moves carefully so as not to crush anything fragile. Crude, awkward, lazy, we might even say foolish, Charles actually proves capable of doing what none of Flaubert's other characters can: loving with maternal selflessness, tender guardianship, and infinite generosity the person he has chosen to love.

Only mothers know how to love this way, asking nothing in return, and who knows whether, in the love between adults, this kind of emotion is not finally deleterious, even catastrophic. In any case, it is without question an emotion that is poetic, meek, magnanimous, splendid.

The evening of *Lucia di Lammermoor*, Emma remains in Rouen with the permission of her husband. The next day she goes to meet Léon in church. She intends at first only to hand him a farewell letter. But while giving it to him, she remains struck by his assertion that he has always loved her and has waited for her all those years.

Once again, it is language that plays the intermediary in love. Emma is swayed neither by force nor by promises. It is only when the other knows how to find "the right words," when he leaps fully into the magic circle of romance novel style, only then does she acknowledge her equal and finally acquiesce.

"'No, my friend, . . . I am too old. . . . You are too young. . . . Forget me!'" Emma says melodramatically. What sexual temptation could rival the pleasure of actually pronouncing such starry literary words?

"Looking tenderly at the young man, she gently repulsed the timid caresses that his trembling hands attempted." This gesture signals yet another of the novel's overtly comic scenes. Flaubert in no way takes his two heroes seriously here, however precisely and naturalistically he has them act out their exchange before us. At the exact same moment in which he is constructing this scene, he is already tearing it down.

It is in this dialectical technique that the greatness of Flaubert's style most probably consists, a style which is spare and realistic and, at the same time, analytic, ironic, abstracted, sharply ideological, and parodic.

Emma so persistently refuses Léon's advances that Léon, out of discretion, decides yet again to give up. But his surrender immediately alarms Emma: "Emma was seized with a vague fear at this shyness, more dangerous to her than the boldness of Rodolphe."

She seems to be performing in a comic scene from the theater of Plautus: he insists; she denies; he desists out of shyness; she is seized with consternation—but how to make him insist again without appearing too shameless? It is all a game of hints and suggestions; as soon as one pulls back, the fun is over.

But Emma, to her discredit, does not take it as just a game. She needs to believe that each of her moves constitutes a specific event, magnificent and fated, in some spectacular tragedy being played upon the stage of life. From the space created between the characters' intentions and the facts of the plot flows a kind of comedy which is mocking, horrible, irresistible.

"No man had ever seemed to her so beautiful. His demeanor suggested an exquisite candor. He lowered his long curling eyelashes. The soft skin of his cheek was flushed, she thought, with desire for her, and Emma felt an invincible longing to press her lips to it."

They leave the church together. Léon calls a carriage. Emma hesitates, says she isn't sure, calls it a thing that "isn't done." Her verbal adherence to the character is perfect. A theater audience would have applauded at length.

Léon, for once, is firm, cutting her short with, "'Everybody does it in Paris!'" "This, like a decisive argument, entirely convinced her," our friend Flaubert, with his usual sniggering cruelty, explains. What could have convinced the little provincial, so falsely modest, if not the mythical image of the city that dictates the laws of behavior and fashion? Molière could not have written the scene any better.

Hence, we come to the famous carriage episode that so greatly scandalized the moralists of the time and that stands today as a masterpiece of literary eros.

And yet even this famous dramatic scene is depicted sarcastically, without a hint of lyricism. In the mere fact of the carriage's randomly chosen route—Léon, as he mounted, having simply said "'Anywhere!'" to the coachman—we can already hear the sardonic laughter of the author. "It went down the Rue Grand-Pont, crossed the Place des Arts, the Quai Napoleon, the Pont Neuf, and stopped short before the statue of Pierre Corneille."

"'Go on,'" cries a voice from within the carriage, almost as soon as the coachman signals the horses to stop. And the cab continues on its crazy course. But, in obeying, the coachman takes too many curves, at which point one again hears that same voice from inside shouting, "'No, straight on!'"

Flaubert never describes what the two inside the coach are doing, but we can certainly imagine. We understand that the curves are somehow disturbing the long embrace of the two and that every stop torments them. We are bothered in the same way when we try to sleep on the train. It is the stops that always awaken us, while the monotonous rocking of the train car in motion lulls us to sleep.

The carriage must stay on its course for the two inside to continue conjoining themselves in whatever way they are. We follow the affair's progress on the face of the driver, who looks increasingly perplexed and annoyed. Only when the horse trots along in a straight line are those two in there satisfied. At each stop, at each curve, one hears a half-suffocated voice that orders: *"Marchez donc!"*

And so things proceed for a good two hours until the driver stops, exhausted, disheartened, and "almost weeping with thirst, fatigue and despair."

Flaubert's comment: "Near the harbor, among the trucks and the barrels, and along the street corners and the sidewalks, bourgeois stared in wonder at this thing unheard of in the provinces: a cab with all blinds drawn that reappeared incessantly, more tightly sealed than a tomb and tossed around like a ship on the waves."

If the two within shared pleasure, deliverance, joy, plenty, caresses, love, kisses, *we* certainly get to see only the most unpleasant and farcical side of their experience: that traveling "tomb" upon which the good burghers of Rouen turn their astounded gaze.

Flaubert's first amorous excursion with Louise also took place in a carriage, after they had met at the house of Pradier the sculptor, who was intent on doing a portrait of her. "But do you know how I keep seeing you? As you were when you were standing in the studio, posing, the light falling on you from the side, when I looked at you and you looked at me" (August 6, 1846). Flaubert invited her to take a carriage ride in the Bois de Boulogne, and she accepted.

On that occasion, however, Louise's young daughter Henriette was also present. Surely the two could not have flirted openly, even if Henriette hadn't been so conveniently "sleeping." Flaubert recalls, "How Henriette was sleeping on the cushions! And the gentle motion of the springs, and our hands and our gazes entwined. I saw your eyes sparkling in the night. My heart was warm and soft" (August 26, 1846).

There was also a second carriage ride, which took place in a manner very similar to the one described in the book. Flaubert ridiculed it some years later during a well-known dinner at the house of the Goncourt brothers: Gustave tells us the story of "screwing La Colet in a carriage while taking her home, and performing for her while he did it the role of the man disgusted by life, dark, mournful, suicidal, a part he enjoyed playing, and which amused him so much that he had to stick his nose out of the window from time to time so he could laugh under his breath" (December 6, 1862).

But let us come back to Emma, who, returning from that famous carriage ride so extraordinarily described by Flaubert, finds that the post chaise to Yonville has already left. What will Charles, who so anxiously awaits her arrival, say? Her heart, as her author says, "felt already that cowardly docility that is for some women at once the chastisement and atonement of adultery."

This sentence contrasts curiously with everything Flaubert has told us up to this point. Hasn't Emma been judged to be insolent, caustic, aggressive? Wasn't it for these reasons that Flaubert so harshly and unrelentingly reproached her? And now, instead, he blames her for her new "cowardly docility." Is this yet another repugnant, contradictory, and unfortunate trait to associate with that "treacherous" creature who responds to the name of Emma?

One morning Léon pays a visit to Homais the pharmacist and casually invites him to visit him in Rouen. Homais takes Léon at his word and shows up at his hotel a few days later, at exactly the time Léon is to meet Emma.

Homais drags him to a restaurant; he bends his ear with vulgar chatter: "The German was romantic, the French woman licentious, the Italian passionate," and so on.

Léon, who is timid and does not dare tell the pharmacist that he has another appointment, manages to escape only after the meal, the coffee, and the ritual smoke. When he arrives at the hotel, Emma is gone. Exasperated by the long wait, she has already left. "His failure to come as he had promised she took as an insult"; she considered him "incapable of heroism, weak, banal, more spiritless than a woman, avaricious, and timorous as well." "But the picking apart of those we love always alienates us from them," Flaubert accurately observes; "One must not touch one's idols, a little of the gilt always comes off on one's fingers."

Had not the same thing happened to Louise, with all of Gustave's missed appointments, his promising her he would meet her in Paris on such-and-such a day, at such-and-such a time, and then, at the last minute, sending her a note to say that he wouldn't be able to come, or simply not showing up?

Louise's resentment certainly built up inside of her, sullying her idol, until her hands became soiled with gold.

"I have received your ["*votre*"] letter from the day before yesterday. Again tears, recrimination, and what is even funnier, insults. And all this because I didn't come to an appointment I never made. You ["*vous*"] will say that there was a tacit understanding between us that I should have been there. But if I was not able to come, if there were reasons for my absence that you ["*vous*"] could not have known[,] . . . it matters not, since you ["*vous*"] worry little enough already about what happens to me" (August 6, 1847).

This change from the familiar *tu* to the more formal *vous* form of address, after nearly a year of amorous connection between them, is difficult to understand—all the more so since in his following letter to her, Flaubert will return to the *tu*. Could it be that he wanted to distance himself from Louise? Or that he feared his mother would look askance at their relationship? Many of his decisions depended on his mother. The fear of provoking her jealousy must have been intense indeed, since young Gustave required Louise to send her letters to Maxime Du Camp, who then inserted them into different envelopes and addressed them to Croisset so that they would appear to be missives from Flaubert's friend.

"You say that one day I will hate you," Louise writes in one of her few surviving letters, "but you do not know me. I have never known hate, and I do not believe, however many changes you suppose my feelings have undergone, that you will ever be able to make me feel an emotion that my whole being revolts against" (November 9, 1847).

In fact, Louise's love for Gustave was tenacious and endured for years, notwithstanding the distance between them, his rudeness, his lack of love for her, the infrequency of their sexual encounters, his expressions of boredom, and his inability to tolerate her behavior. "Oh what joy, to have found Gustave again," she wrote in her diary after their reconciliation in 1851; "However indifferent his feelings toward me, I will not be affrighted by this. I love him more than anyone else, and he too appreciates me. And then all of these severed relations are so harmful, they humiliate me."

Emma, too, has an extraordinary capacity to "forgive" the lover who neglects her, and she returns to Léon "more avid and inflamed than before."

By now Emma's adultery has become second nature. She no longer displays those attitudes of false modesty and feigned reticence that she had deemed so essential to the proper behavior of a "true lady." When she enters the hotel room, she immediately undresses and, completely naked, throws herself bodily upon Léon with a theatrical flair.

Louise also made love with great eagerness and exaggerated abandon. Flaubert was clearly frightened by this: "Do not love me so much, you hurt me! Let me love you! Don't you know that to love excessively brings bad luck to lover and beloved? It's like overfondled children: they die young. Life is not made for that; happiness is a monstrosity; they who seek it are punished" (August 9, 1846).

"Yesterday, I brought my daughter to Dr. Toirac," wrote Louise in her diary, "He spoke to me of Gustave. Of his leaving for the Orient in a few days. He will depart without seeing me, without writing me. Inexplicable heart! Mine would like to cease beating and feeling. The pain is too great" (September 28, 1849).

"You may think that I am an egoist and afraid of you," Flaubert wrote to her, "Well, I am. Your love overwhelms me because I feel that it is devouring us both, you particularly. You are like Ugolino in prison, devouring your own flesh to appease your hunger" (August 9, 1846).

Years later, he wrote: "I am afraid, poor dear Louise, of hurting you (though it is good that in our arrangement nothing is hidden between us), but do not send me your photographic portrait. I detest photographs as much as I love their originals. . . . Ah, how old I am, how old I am, poor dear Louise" (August 14, 1853).

And again: "I love you very much when I see you are calm and working well. I love you even more, perhaps, when I know you are suffering. And then you write me letters full of such spirit. But, poor dear soul, control yourself! Try to moderate your 'southern temper,' as you say, speaking of Ferrat" (June 28, 1853).

"Your voice is filled with sobs, and I hear nothing but the cries of your pain accusing me. Your poor soul is like a wounded warrior. Wherever one tries to hold it, one touches a wound and hurts you" (October 24, 1846).

"There was . . . in those wild eyes [of Emma's]," Flaubert writes, "something strange, vague and sinister that seemed to Léon to be subtly gliding between them to force them apart."

"Finding how experienced she was, [Léon] told himself that she must have passed through all the extremes of both pleasure and pain. What had once charmed now frightened him a little." He feels himself caught, absorbed by her as if she wanted to devour him.

"He resented her because of this constant victory," Flaubert writes of Léon, seemingly writing about himself: "He even strove not to love her; then, when he heard the creaking of her boots, he felt his courage desert him, like drunkards at the sight of strong liquor."

Emma, on the other hand, "showered him with every sort of attention. . . . She used to bring roses from Yonville hidden in her bosom which she would toss up into his face; she was worried about his health, advised him how he should behave; and in order to bind him closer to her, hoping perhaps that heaven would take her part, she hung a medal of the Virgin round his neck."

Louise possessed this same mania for gift giving, always bringing something new for Gustave: flowers, embroidered pillows, paperweights, bonbons. Gustave scolded her. He felt that those gifts were intended to put him under obligations of gratitude. They were offerings to an angry god to beseech his benevolence.

But Louise understood that obscure fetishism that Flaubert so willingly gave himself up to. Had he not saved and hidden, from the very first days of their affair, certain secret treasures: the blue slippers, the handkerchief stained with blood, the lock of hair in the portrait, the little bag of letters ("I reread [them] and breathe their musky perfume"), not to mention the famous "cigarette case with the inscription '*Amor nel cor*'"?

Flaubert loved to surround himself with souvenirs: "I never sell my old clothes. Sometimes I go up to the attic where I keep them and look at them, and I think about when they were new and all the things I did when I was wearing them" (August 8–9, 1846).

Like Louise, Emma also loves to shower her beloved with little souvenir gifts that she hoped would become fetish objects. These gifts were, moreover, a testament to her happiness—a happiness, however, that was far from being an emotional reality for her. "'I do love him!'" Emma says to herself. But this is not enough for her. "Why was her life so unsatisfactory," Flaubert asks himself, "Why did everything she leaned on rot and give way?"

We find almost the exact same words in one of Louise's first letters: "We are nothing but alternating corruption and putrefaction, constantly interspersed with each other" (December 13, 1846).

"Everything was a lie," Emma says to herself. "Every smile concealed a yawn of boredom, every joy a curse, every pleasure its own disgust, and the sweetest kisses left upon your lips only the unattainable desire for a greater delight."

These are all concepts that we recognize from the most sincere letters that passed between Gustave and Louise, and which belong to the recurrent theme of taedium vitae in Flaubert. "Everything about life repels me; everything that draws me into its abyss appalls me. . . . There is in me, deep down, a bitter, ceaseless and fundamental *exasperation*, which prevents my enjoying anything, and fills my mind to bursting point. It turns up on any occasion, like the bloated bodies of dogs that rise to the surface, whatever stones one has tied round their necks to drown them" (December 20, 1846).

"It is pitiful, but I've always been this way, continuously craving what I don't have and not knowing how to enjoy it when I do have it, and so I get distressed and frighten myself with prophecies of doom" (December 7, 1846).

"I was born bored, this is the leprosy which consumes me. I am bored with life, with myself, with others, with everything" (December 2, 1846).

As Gustave, so now Emma. Notwithstanding her love—or perhaps precisely because of its too great, too overwhelming, intensity—she becomes aware of the sweetish taste of death on her tongue, and she obsessively asks herself why she is the way she is.

ᴥ᚜᚛ᴥ

Emma Bovary is distressed about her lack of money. But instead of trying to cut back on her expenses, she throws herself into making more and more costly and unnecessary purchases, falling deeper into debt to the ever present, ever greedy Monsieur Lheureux, who continues to let her sign one promissory note after another. The money is eaten up by trips to Rouen, hotels for amorous encounters, gifts, flowers, restaurants.

Here we might well be watching Louise, another woman in constant anxiety over a lack of money. She was too proud, however, to ask for any from the old philosopher, Victor Cousin, who had been her lover for years and whom she believed, though without complete certainty, to be the father of her daughter. She was absolutely unable to appeal to her new lover, Gustave Flaubert, for help. He, for his part, barely seemed to notice her reduced circumstances, nor did he offer to assist her in her more difficult moments. "Gustave is kind, generous," Louise wrote, "rather lavish in his spending, but he is by no means concerned for the humiliations which harry the woman he has passionately grasped in his arms. . . . I have only ten francs left for all of the next trimester."

"I've found my peace of mind again, having regained Gustave's affection; it's not everything, but it sustains me. I need to work, and if work could make me finally independent of the Philosopher for the care of my daughter, I would be completely happy."

Louise's attempt to earn money through literature was pathetic. Only professional writers who churned out a novel every six months were able, with great difficulty, to support themselves as authors. In fact, Louise was forced to write boring society chronicles for newspapers and to do translations, which payed terribly. Her need to be independent, like Emma's, was wedded to the world of her dreams. Poverty, however, was concrete, defined by periodic debts and by her dependence upon the men she had chosen to love, which in turn provoked resentment, because it provoked in her a feeling of impotence. Not knowing which party to petition for help, she finally decided to ask Gustave for a loan. He advanced her five hundred francs. She repaid the loan almost immediately, though in installments.

"Emma lived all absorbed in her passions and worried no more

89

about money matters than an archduchess," Flaubert writes of his heroine.

In the meanwhile, Lheureux threatens to take Emma to court to make her pay back her debts; Emma begs him not to do it, and he presses her to sign more promissory notes.

At the insistent urging of the merchant, Emma asks her husband for money. Penniless himself, he in turn asks his mother for some, and she writes him that she has nothing left and that she has already advanced him his entire inheritance.

Emma begins to sell off objects from around the house, "bargain[ing] rapaciously." This "rapaciously" is an especially gratuitous insult. Hasn't Flaubert just suggested that, in her passionate absorption, she was as incapable of worrying about money as an archduchess? How does he reconcile this rapaciousness with an archduchess's prodigality?

"Her peasant blood [stood] her in good stead. . . . She borrowed from Félicité, from Madame Lefrançois, from the landlady at the 'Croix Rouge,' from everybody, no matter where." But since Emma spends all this money on gifts, it is difficult to think of her as greedy.

She sometimes forces herself to sit down and add up her accounts, but, Flaubert writes, "the results were always so staggering, she couldn't believe they were possible. Then she would begin over again, soon get confused, leave everything where it was and forget about it."

The Bovary household begins to take on a run-down appearance: tradesmen can be seen brusquely leaving it with annoyed looks on their faces. And little Berthe "wore stockings with holes in them."

If Charles timidly dares to make some remark, Emma responds rudely, "savagely," that it isn't her fault and that he should leave her alone. Charles, the one character who evinces a completely disinterested generosity, worries first and foremost about Emma and their child. That child, Berthe of the stockings with holes in them, would ask where her mother was, and he would gently answer: "'Go call your nurse. . . . You know, my darling, that mama does not like to be disturbed!'"

But what is this mama who does not like to be disturbed doing? She is alone in her bedroom, half-dressed, "lighting a tablet of Turkish incense she had bought at the shop of an Algerian in Rouen."

Algerian shops, incense tablets, belts, and silks were also a passion of Flaubert's, and they formed part of his desire for the exotic that he judged so contemptible and ridiculous in his heroine.

So as not to find her husband beside her in bed, Emma manages "by continual badgering to relegate him to a room on the third floor," Flaubert writes. This way, she can read until morning.

We ask ourselves what it is that Emma, at this point in her life, can be reading. Still the same sentimental novels and romances of adventure? No, her books, as Flaubert tells us, have become "lurid." In them can be found "scenes of orgies, violence and bloodshed." Sometimes, Emma would be "seized by a sudden terror and cry out." Charles would run to her side; "'Oh! Leave me alone!'" she would snap.

"Or at other times, when she was burnt more fiercely by that inner flame which her adultery kept feeding, panting and overcome with desire, she would throw open the window breathing in the chill air and letting the wind blow back her hair which hung too heavy on her neck, and, looking up at the stars, she would long for the love of a prince."

Incurable, our Emma. After everything that has happened to her, she still "long[s] for the love of a prince." It is as if she has not banged her head hard enough on the walls of reality, as if she has not already drunk the wine of illicit love to the bitter dregs.

One day, not having enough money to pay for a hotel room, Emma hands Léon six small silver-gilt spoons that had been a wedding gift from her father and begs her lover to pawn them for her. Léon obeys, however reluctantly, but "began to think that his mistress was beginning to behave rather strangely, and perhaps they were not wrong in wishing to separate him from her."

Léon's mother, it turns out, has received an anonymous letter saying that her son is "'ruining himself with a married woman.'" "The good woman had visions of the eternal bug-a-boo of every family, that is to say, that vague and terrible creature, the siren, the fantastic monster which makes its home in the treacherous depths of love." She writes to Léon's employer, who sends for his employee and asks him to break off "an intrigue [which] would damage him later on in his career." By the end of this meeting, Léon promises not to see the "woman" anymore. But, in fact, he continues to see her clandestinely and plagued now by guilt.

In a more genteel and thoughtful way, Léon makes the same kinds of calculations as Rodolphe: he will become "head clerk" before long, so there is no point in wasting his energies on improper love affairs. "Every bourgeois," as Flaubert comments, "in the flush of his youth, were it but for a day, a moment, has believed himself capable of immense passions, of lofty enterprises."

We know from his letters what Flaubert thinks of the bourgeoisie. His critique of them is incessant and irate: "And here is a fossil I am beginning to understand well (the bourgeois)! What half-characters, half-wills, half-passions. How everything in their brains fluctuates, is uncertain and weak! Oh practical men, men of action, prudent men, how incompetent, asleep, limited I find you!" (August 16, 1853).

This was possibly the only reproach—that of being bourgeois—with which Gustave never charged Louise, and it was for this, perhaps, that he loved her, when he loved her.

In the novel, meanwhile, Emma is becoming more and more unbalanced. In the middle of lovemaking she breaks out in hiccups or in sudden, sinister laughter. She talks to herself, attacks her dear Léon, scolding him, haranguing him.

"His heart, like the people who can only stand a certain amount of music, became drowsy through indifference to the vibrations of a love whose subtleties he could no longer distinguish," Flaubert says of Léon.

Not that Emma isn't, at least a bit, conscious of how tiresome their love has become. "Emma found again in adultery all the platitudes of marriage."

Now Léon too, like Rodolphe before him, racks his brains over "how to get rid of" her. Get rid of her, that is, without too much public embarrassment, without making her suffer too much, without staining his reputation as a man of honor, without provoking her senseless wrath.

Coldness, distance, a harsh word are not enough. Emma shouts and storms, laying claim to her rights as a lover, and it is impossible for him to escape her.

The same anxieties plagued young Flaubert: how to get rid of Louise without provoking those stormy rages which threatened to overwhelm him? How to distance himself from her without her broadcasting all over Paris what a brute he was? How, without mortally wounding her, for which he would have felt guilty for years afterward?

"You love me yet. Thank you for so much love," he wrote in a letter of January 15, 1847, after they had known each other for only a year: "Such things can fill an avid heart to overflowing. There are some treasures before which one sits, melancholy, thinking that one is not worthy of them."

"I would have wanted to love you as you loved me. I hurled myself in vain against the fatality of my nature, nothing, nothing. . . . Loving, above all, tranquility and repose, I found in you nothing but upheaval, storms, tears, or rage. Once you pouted because I told the carriage driver to take you home, and what a scene you made at dinner with Max, and what a fury you were in at the station because I did not come to meet you! . . . But I won't reproach you. It was not in your power to prevent all this from happening to me, just as it was not in my power not to suffer from it . . . sentimentally and intellectually. . . . The scenes that you made at Du Camp's house and at the hotel, where you took yourself to see if I had left, made me look extremely ridiculous. I possess the weakness of loving decorum. . . . Oh, why, and why yet again, did you ever come to know me? What sin, poor woman, are you expiating? Surely you deserved better than this" (March 7, 1847).

It seems strange to hear Flaubert speaking of "decorum." But, at this point, any excuse might have served to stem the flow of Louise's passions. At the same time, Flaubert mixed such sympathy with brutal honesty: "Your ideas of morality, of country, of dedication, your literary tastes, all of this is antithetical to my ideas and my tastes. . . . You wanted to squeeze blood from a stone. You barely nicked the stone and you bloodied your finger" (March 7, 1847).

Even Emma Bovary realizes, notwithstanding her ongoing recriminations and her amorous aggressiveness toward Léon, that their love is no longer a true one. "Though she felt humiliated by the sordidity of such a happiness, she clung to it out of habit, or out of degeneration."

The idea of Emma's "degeneration" reappears with increasing frequency in the text as we get closer to the ending, as if to prepare the reader for the brutal punishment that will be inflicted on her.

The reader would not be able to accept the viciousness of Emma's final punishment if Emma had not already reached the bottom of what Flaubert calls her "depravity." And by this word he means not simply her adultery but also her exploration, more and more complacent and even arrogant, of pleasure and freedom.

It is at this juncture that the novel's misinterpretation by male, rather than female, readers is born. Emma Bovary, notwithstanding her notoriously wicked character and inane reading habits, perseveres in her tenacious, underground dream of liberty. And she senses that such liberty consists, first and foremost, in sexual disobedience.

It is as if Emma knows, in the depths of her seething heart, that the most essential component of her whole enterprise is the desire which animates her female body. That desire, however distorted, diseased, deformed, incomplete, and larval, removes itself, by its mere existence, from the control exerted upon it by a culture determined to regulate human reproduction and sexual pleasure. Emma, therefore, carries within herself the germ of rebellion.

Curious destiny, that of Flaubert! Detesting every form of literature that takes the part of the outraged, the forsaken, the undefended, he nevertheless wound up the spokesman (against his will and resisting at every step) for an archetype of female freedom. The obscure engine of adultery, Emma Bovary seems to tell us, powers—and vindicates—a crude and primitive politics of female sexual liberation in a world that prescribes its negotiated submission.

Throughout the entire narrative, Emma makes bungling attempts to validate just those ideas that Flaubert systematically condemns, dissipates, scorns. But the power of Emma's rebellion, pathetic and pigheaded as it is, manages to bubble up from beneath the mountains of derision that bury it, almost contrary to Flaubert's intentions. The popularity of the book with female readers of the last century and with those of today derives, I believe, from this: the keen sympathy that Emma's struggle still elicits, after all is said and done.

E mma has learned by now to "degenerately" split herself in two. While she continues to write Léon a letter every day, she thinks of other things, pursues old and new "phantoms."

These ghosts "became so real, so tangible, that her heart beat wildly in awe and admiration." These are fleeting, confused, and attractive phantoms, "fashioned out of her most ardent memories . . . that dwelt in that azure land where silken ladders swung from balconies in the moonlight, beneath a flower-scented breeze."

This image of phantoms was based on a curious minor event in Gustave and Louise's relationship. She must certainly not have been very happy to find the idea utilized, in however modified a form, in Flaubert's novel.

The facts—or, rather, the premises—are these: Louis Bouilhet had sent Louise Colet one of his poems, which he had dedicated to her, praising her "white arms and golden hair." Louise excitedly sent the poem to Gustave, simultaneously forwarding a copy also to the review *L'Artiste* so that it could be published.

As soon as he read Bouilhet's poem, Flaubert flew into a rage. He wrote a furious letter of entreaty to the beautiful Louise: "Don't let that poem be published. I am asking you as a favor to me. And here are the reasons: it would cover the both of you with ridicule. The hack writers with nothing better to do would leap to make fun of those 'gazes of flame,' those 'white arms,' that 'genius,' and above all that 'the queen.' That 'do not you touch the queen' would become proverbial. . . . If they were good verses, at least . . . ; but the fact is that they are truly mediocre (I had read them, and I talked to you about them). You yourself were revolted by that mixing of the physical and the moral that I find here so excessive and clumsy. . . . Beyond the brief moment of glory, it would do you serious harm. . . . He and I have agreed that he will write you another, more serious and publishable. . . . I urge you to reconsider, I even implore you to" (September 1, 1852).

Louise immediately contacted *L'Artiste* to stop them from publishing Bouilhet's poem. Luckily, she intervened in time: the poem was not printed, as Flaubert had wished.

The relationship between Louise, Gustave, and Louis touched some strange highs and lows. Gustave was inclined, by his very nature, to "put together" the objects of his affection. In the first phase of Gustave's relationship with Louise, Maxime Du Camp also came to be involved—even came, in a way, to be coopted against his will, invited to serve as mediator, as companion, as emotional buffer.

However, in retrospect, one would say that, all things considered, Louis Bouilhet was far kinder to Louise, while Maxime Du Camp demonstrated a real taste for cruelty toward her. We can see how permeated his letters to her are with an incessant, cynical desire to hurt her feelings.

"Do not tell me that I am cold and hard—more than anything else, I am honest: I prefer to hurt you rather than deceive you: your future happiness may depend on your conduct today. . . . Do not expect him for at least fifteen days. . . . *Adieu*, good and poor sister, be calm, courageous, and patient, and above all work: your last word is sadly true, you love him too much" (December 18, 1846).

"Your first letter, which Gustave showed me, was dignified, calm, and you should have adhered to it." "Be courageous and listen: (1st) he has affection for you: a heartfelt friendship, but that is all, I believe; (2nd) he is capable of great sacrifices for you, but he will never agree to distance himself from his own occupations, not even for a single hour; (3rd) he has been, I believe, deeply wounded by the exaggerated pronouncements you made about his *November*. Not because he believed that you wanted to make fun of it, but because he profoundly admires *René*,[10] to which, quite deservedly, he considers *November* greatly inferior. Before *René* one bows as before a great masterpiece of the human spirit. (4th) He has informed me that he will come to Paris only to see the Salon, that he will stay two days and then depart. In fine, I must tell you that the SOLE means of maintaining some relationship with him is to hold fast to that friendship, that camaraderie that you have established: this is as pleasing to his tastes and to his habits as other emotions are foreign to them" (January 3, 1847).

"I intended to write you these things, dear sister: (1st) that Gustave came several times, and that he stopped to see me; (2nd) that, if I may be permitted to give you some more advice, I would tell you not to see him by any means; this would be the best way

10. *René* (1802), by Francois René de Chateaubriand, one of the seminal works of French Romanticism.

97

to most quickly heal your wounded heart—if, that is, you indeed care to heal it; (3rd) that if you wish to have Gustave near you again for some time, it would be best not to reproach him in any way and, above all, not to cry in front of him: he is, in this respect, like all other men, he does not love recriminations and he detests tears; he wants more than anything else to enjoy himself, and the most certain means of holding on to him is to in no way reveal your sadness to him" (February 16, 1847).

"You accuse me again of hurting you—I do not understand why: I believed myself, in your best interest, to be giving you two or three pieces of advice. . . . You believe me to be false and a liar (perhaps Gustave is already there with you, you say to me); one day, poor sister, you will recognize that I have always been right, and that if you had followed my advice you would not be suffering today what you are suffering" (February 16, 1847).

"I gave no such order to leave you outside my door. . . . I had no idea that you would come. . . . If I had known that it was your intention to come to see me, I would have been sure to prevent the concierge from letting you up—a pointless precaution, really, since no woman has ever set foot in my house. . . . Here is the compendium of Gustave's life in Paris: he arrived Wednesday evening; Thursday we were out together all day attending to matters of money, matters so important that I abandoned everything else in order to help him; Friday he came at nine in the morning to visit with me for ten minutes and to recount the death of poor Félix. . . . You saw him at six; then he went to Mme D'Arcet's house, then he came to my house at eleven or thereabouts, and ten minutes after he arrived he had an attack on my bed: I do not fault you for it, my poor sister, but the attack was solely caused, I am sadly convinced, by what had occurred between you two; at three in the morning I brought him to his hotel; Saturday I took care of him and watched over him all day long, and I must confess that he did not want to hear of coming to visit you today. . . . He left because he feared having another crisis today, Sunday. What had angered him beyond all else in your encounter of Friday was your claim that he had lied. It is an unforgiveable accusation—his pride and his heart have been mortally and irreparably wounded by this suspicion; how could you have accused him of lying, he whose honesty with you has been at times even brutal? . . . Above all, Gustave, as you know, is the man of Plasticity, and you show him nothing but a face disfigured by tears; he loves harmony, and every time you meet him your beauty is contracted in grimaces of weeping and your spirit and your heart are full of nothing but reproof, at times unjust. . . . I do not want to gloat, but I told you so. . . . Now it is too late, and I no longer know what to say, what to do, to sweeten a bit the irremediable evils that you have inflicted upon both of you. Gustave has no love for the sentiment of love, he is tired of it, he is gorged on it. As he told you, he himself has suffered too much to feel any pity for the sufferings of others. He is one of those coldly inflexible men who never go back on a decision once taken, and it is a great misfortune for you to ever have met him at the house of Phidias. He has left Paris, saddened, exasperated, sick, and full of a blind and concentrated anger that frightened me; I had never seen him in such a state; his heart now is full of tumult—it must be left to regain its composure. It would be best for the two of you to remain apart, if I may give you a suggestion. . . . Wait a year before you see him again, and write him only occasionally. . . . If you had let yourself be guided by me, I would have created between you an unbreakable bond. . . . But you wanted, at all costs, to let his love die: trapped in a burning hothouse, the poor plant could not endure the heat and shriveled up" (February 21, 1847).

And finally, in December, an exultant Maxime Du Camp wrote to his friend Gustave: "I sent your letter to the Muse. She sent yours to me. It is sublime[,] . . . exactly how I had imagined it. You did well, excellently well. Life would have been an unending pain in the ass with that woman" (December 27, 1847). Du Camp wrote this shortly after Gustave's first breakup with Louise.

Louis Bouilhet proved to be much kinder than Du Camp. His tone was more concerned, more supportive, even if it was accompanied by perfectly understandable flashes of impatience.

Bouilhet was grateful to Louise because she had been one of the first to secure him a positive review in the newspapers. Bouilhet wrote poetry and plays, and this review had been one of the reasons for the rapprochement between Louise and Flaubert. "I am grateful to you; you are generous," he wrote her in 1851, when they had begun to see each other again after four years of estrangement.

Bouilhet knew Gustave from the time they were boys together, as we have seen. Between them there was a deep and enduring friendship. Gustave wanted to constantly have him by his side in Croisset. They spent the afternoons and evenings together correcting one another's writing.

Each of them had a sexual life apart from their friendship, both with women. They spoke of these women together with typically masculine complicitousness. They sometimes exchanged them, "gave" them to each other as gifts, boasted of them to each other. However, not one of these women, they felt, not for any possible reason in the world, would be allowed to fracture their friendship, the bond they considered to be deeper and more solid than any other.

Having erred in forwarding Bouilhet's poem to Flaubert, Louise sent Flaubert a poem of her own, entitled *"Fantômes,"* which speaks of past loves as literary phantoms, at whose sight "her heart beat wildly in awe and admiration." These ghosts are recognizable in the same "moonlight" that Flaubert attributes to Emma's fantasies.

To exact revenge after he read Bouilhet's too naive and complimentary poem, Flaubert took *"Fantômes"* and destroyed it with gusto, making use of it, however, to vent his anger upon his heroine in *Madame Bovary*.

"The idea was good," he wrote to Louise, "and the beginning is magisterial!* . . . But you heedlessly exhausted it. . . . It must be completely rewritten. . . . In other words, your poem is as broad at the beginning as all humanity and as narrow at the end as the distance between two clamped thighs. . . . I liked almost nothing about the last part" (September 1, 1852).

*Maraini interpolates here several lines from Colet's poem:

She watched the silent line
of beloved images pass,
which, walking toward her,
their eyes and hers meeting,
reminded her of the enflamed hours.

One evening Emma decides to go with Léon and his friends to a masked ball. For the occasion, she dons a pair of velvet pants, red stockings, and a peruke. "She danced all night to the wild sounds of the trombones . . . [with] people gathered around her." Toward daybreak, she finds herself with the few remaining partygoers, by now quite drunk, and among a few women of "the lowest class," smoking and drinking punch. At this moment, she turns her tired gaze upon herself and realizes that her clothes are rumpled, that she's woozy, and that she has taken on the appearance of a girl of easy virtue. She is overwhelmed by shame, which takes the form of an irrepressible rage against herself.

But, however sincere she may be here, she is unable, as Flaubert tells us, to avoid her usual melodramatic tone. "She would have liked to take wing like a bird, and fly off far away to become young again in the realms of immaculate purity." And while he writes this, he smokes a last scented cigarette.

Here, again, we find the theme of androgyny in the novel linked to nocturnal eroticism, to sensual indulgence, and, far from accidentally, to a suggestion of vice, of depravity. In order to fully enjoy the ball Emma dresses as a man, and that transvestism expresses all the melancholy of someone who desires power but lacks the means to obtain it. To us, she simply seems pathetic, the way those who want but cannot get, whose eyes are bigger than their stomachs, who pretend to be something they can never be, seem pathetic.

The next morning, a warrant to repossess the furniture arrives at the Bovarys'. The doctor must pay the sum of eight thousand francs within twenty-four hours. This is an enormous amount, one which very few Yonvilleans would have on hand—least of all one like Charles Bovary, a small municipal doctor who cannot even get his patients to pay him.

Emma receives the injunction while her husband is out. Thinking she can remedy the situation before he returns, she rushes off to see Lheureux. "'It's a joke, I'm sure!'" she angrily says to him. He coldly replies that it isn't, that this time she will have to pay.

"She turned coward; she implored him; she even pressed her pretty white and slender hand against the shopkeeper's knee." He pulls sharply away from her. "'There, that'll do! Any one'd think you wanted to seduce me!'" he says maliciously.

"'You are a wretch!'" she screamed at him, "'I'll tell my husband . . .'" "'I too, I'll show your husband something!'" he shoots back, and pulls from his pocket a note for eighteen hundred francs that she had signed.

This is one of the harshest of the scenes depicting Emma's behavior. Flaubert knows it and seems quite happy to vilify her: the request for an umpteenth postponement, accompanied by a seduction attempt; the "pretty white and slender hand" placed on the knee of the hateful merchant; his refusal; the immediate, indignant offense she takes; her slandered virtue and her threat to take the matter to her husband—which provokes Lheureux's ill will, this time justifiable.

Emma comes out of the encounter discredited, more severely than ever: false, cowardly, vengeful, lying, ready to dally with even the repugnant Lheureux so as to extract yet another postponement from him. What next?

This is the Flaubertian idea that reappears time and again in the novel—that Emma is worthy of condemnation not for betraying her husband but for her vulgar nature, for her cold and self-centered pursuit of a kind of pleasure that not even she understands, for her stupid attachment to the most inane of literary myths, for her dime-store sentimentalism.

One wonders whether, despite all his assurances (always made out of both sides of his mouth) of the esteem in which he held her, Flaubert did not have the same plainly disparaging opinion of Louise Colet that he has of Emma.

Yet it was precisely in letters he sent to Louise during the second phase of their relationship—those in which he constantly referred to her as "poor soul," "poor dear," and "my poor woman"—that he wrote of *Madame Bovary*. "I believe this is the first time that a book has ever made sport of both the young heroine and her young leading man. The irony will take nothing away from the pathos. It will magnify it instead. In the third section, which will be full of farcical moments, I want to make people cry" (October 9, 1852).

"Frankly, there are moments in which I almost feel like I want to vomit, physically, so deep is the bottom" of *Madame Bovary* (April 13, 1853). "*Saint Antoine* didn't demand a quarter of the mental tension that *Bovary* is causing me. It was an outlet for my feelings; I had only pleasure in writing it. . . . Think of me now: having constantly to be in the skins of people for whom I feel aversion" (April 6, 1853).

When the day the furniture is to be repossessed is finally at hand, we see officials of the court arriving at the Bovary household to inventory the individual pieces along with some other objects. Emma faces them "stoical[ly]." But she is still convinced, in her dreamer's brain, that she will somehow be able to rectify matters and hide everything from her husband. As soon as the officials have left, in fact, she rushes off to Rouen to look for someone who will extend credit to her. The two bankers she meets with, however, politely send her packing.

Not knowing whom else to ask, Emma swallows her pride and goes to see Léon. She embraces him, kisses him, makes him believe that she has come simply to visit him, and then suddenly tells him that she needs, immediately, eight thousand francs. "'But you are mad!'" he replies. She explains to him that her husband knows nothing yet, that the creditors are returning in a few hours, and that if she does not find the money all is lost. Only he can help her.

"'But what do you want me . . . ?'" Léon worriedly asks. To which she immediately snaps, "'What a coward you are!'" She finally convinces him to go and scrape together at least three thousand francs, making him understand that this is his duty as a lover. "'Where?'" he asks, dismayed. "'At your office,'" she resolutely responds. He pales at the suggestion. "A diabolical determination showed in her burning eyes which were half closed in a lascivious and encouraging manner." Emma, that is, urges Léon to steal for her, and from his place of work at that.

At this point Léon is truly terrified, but he is unable to react honestly. Therefore, he proceeds cunningly, by telling her that, yes, perhaps he does have a friend who can lend him some money, that he will try, he will do it, but that "'if you don't see me by three o'clock, do not wait for me.'"

Emma returns to Yonville dejected, after having waited over three hours, cursing Léon's cowardliness. She finds posters on the city walls announcing the sale of her furniture. But she refuses to admit defeat. There is still Guillaumin the notary, she says to herself, why had she not thought of him earlier! He is a friend of both Lheureux's and Charles's, he will surely help her.

One of Emma's traits, like that of Louise before her, is an inability to understand her fellow human beings. Her instincts unfailingly lead her to the wrong person at the wrong time, prevent her from sensing someone's tone, cause her to take apples for oranges. This is because, as Flaubert suggests, instead of looking people in the face, she looks them "in the heart," or, rather, in some abstracted notion of it—heart with a capital *H*.

Emma bursts into the darkened house of *maître* Guillaumin and finds him eating a cutlet and drinking a cup of tea. Dispensing with the formalities, she immediately asks him for a loan of three thousand francs. He looks at her curiously. He says neither yes nor no. Meanwhile, "he held out his hand, took hers, kissed it greedily, then held it on his knee; and he played delicately with her fingers, while muttering thousands of compliments."

At this point Emma, after initially obliging (she leaves her hand resting on the notary's knee so he can caress her fingers), suddenly changes her tone and reacts harshly. Perhaps she is afraid of repeating the error she had made with Lheureux. Or perhaps it is that this time it is not she who seduces but he who propositions, and this makes her feel insulted rather than flattered. Or perhaps, once again, it is the pleasure of the performance above all that she craves (Flaubert has us understand that, at bottom, this is the real reason). Whatever the case, she pulls away from him indignantly. While pulling away, she repeats her request for money, more arrogantly than before. But the notary, still stunned by her abrupt about-face, falls to his knees saying, "'I beg you, stay! I love you!'" Then he puts his arms around her waist and tries to kiss her. But Emma again slips aside, and "with a terrible look" shouts, "'I am to be pitied—not to be sold.'"

This scene greatly resembles a story that Louise recounted to Flaubert in a letter now lost, a story he took up and analyzed in his sarcastic response. The event narrated by Louise was this: Alfred de Musset, who had for some time been trying to court Louise, invited her one day to take a carriage ride with him. During the ride, he attempted to force himself on her. She tried to repel him but was unsuccessful, so she opened the carriage door and leaped out with the carriage going at full speed, risking a broken neck in the process. The following day, all battered and bruised, she wrote to Flaubert about the episode. Flaubert justifiably waxes indignant: "I would beat his brains out with great pleasure," he says of de Musset. "If he so much as steps on my foot, I will kick him in the stomach with it. . . . Ah, my poor Louise, I imagined you for a moment dead upon the road with the wheel of the carriage rolling over your stomach and the horse's hoof crushing your face. . . . Oh, how I wish that he would show up again at your house so that you could kick him out publicly before me and thirty others. If he comes looking for you again, write him a *monumental* letter of five lines: 'Why do I no longer wish to see you? Because you disgust me and you are vile. . . . ' You, however, lacked some tact in this affair. There is air in women's heads like the air in the chamber of a double bass. Instead of leaping from the moving carriage, you should have addressed the driver and said, 'Do me the pleasure of throwing out this Monsieur Alfred de Musset who insults me'" (July 7, 1852).

This tact, however, would not have been in the nature of Louise, who at one point, enraged by an article that offended her, stealthily entered the home of the journalist Alphonse Karr and flew at him, brandishing a knife. Naturally, she was so reckless and such a bungler that the journalist was easily able to disarm her and put her out, the next day spreading the story all over Paris.

After receiving the letter from her beloved Gustave, Louise thought (exactly as Emma would have in such a situation) that she must prevent a duel between the two. She wrote to Flaubert at once, begging him to "not be enraged."

In response to her concern, Flaubert only offered sarcasm: "Why do you seem to be begging me not to kill him, as if I were some kind of Rodomonte[11] and had used bellicose expressions[?] . . . Be assured that I have no intention of looking for an occasion to fight" (July 12, 1852).

11. Rodamonte, the ferocious and swaggering warrior in Matteo Maria Boiardo's *Orlando Innamorato* (1495), later appears as Rodomonte in Ludovico Ariosto's *Orlando Furioso* (1532).

What Louise did not write to Flaubert was that she and Alfred de Musset had already made love and that they saw each other often. They often fought, however, because he drank too much, and when he drank he grew rude and aggressive and was gripped by a desire to rape her. Once, as she relates in her diary, returning from a ride in the Bois, he had made the driver stop the carriage at the tap-room at least three times so he could drink absinthe.

ut let us return to Emma, standing in the dining room of Guillaumin the notary, who is on his knees before her as she pulls
indignantly away from him.

At this point, we recall, Flaubert puts words in her mouth that
could not be more theatrical or artificial: "'I am to be pitied—not
to be sold.'" We can almost hear the fanfare of trumpets! Who
could believe in her genuineness at this moment when, just a short
while ago, it had been *she* who attempted to "sell herself" to the
merchant Lheureux (preserving the forms, of course) so as not to
have to pay her debts? Poor Emma, with no respite from Flaubert's
implacable judgment, can never show herself to be the slightest
bit humane.

And yet, some readers of the time approved Emma's theatrical
refusal as a duty properly discharged, a sign of the protagonist's
moral revolt against mistreatment and blackmail. But such readers
did not take into account the author, who, standing in a corner, observes the entire scene with a skeptical eye and explains to us that
"the disappointment of her failure increased the indignation of
her outraged modesty; it seemed to her that Providence pursued
her implacably, and, strengthening herself in her pride, she had
never felt so much esteem for herself nor so much contempt for
others. A spirit of warfare transformed her. She would have liked
to strike all men, to spit in their faces, to crush them."

Flaubert's animosity toward the spirit of womanly revenge, so
dear to his friend Louise, came out clearly in his letters to her:
"You tell me . . . that women are not free. . . . It's true. We teach
them to lie regularly, and we tell them many lies as well. *And no
one is ever able to tell them the truth.* When one has the misfortune
of being frank with them, they get annoyed by such strange behavior. What I blame them for most of all is their need to poeti-
cize everything. If a man loves a servant girl, he may know that
this is stupid, but that won't prevent him from enjoying her. But if
a woman makes love with any old clod, she transforms him immediately into a misunderstood genius, one of the chosen ones"
(April 24, 1852).

And again, responding to Louise's complaints and egalitarian
enthusiasms, he wrote: "Women are not honest with themselves.
. . . They take their ass for their heart and believe the moon sits in

107

the sky to illuminate their boudoirs. They completely lack cynicism, which is the irony of vice, and if by chance they do possess it, it is an affectation. The courtesan is a myth. No woman has ever invented any dissolute thing. The heart of women is a piano that man, egotistical artist that he is, loves to play tunes upon to make himself shine, every key singing of him" (April 24, 1852).

Today, of course, it would be easy to attribute the flaws Flaubert names to the faults of the period, to conditions of female dependence, and so to the "hysteria" of a female prisoner. But Flaubert, like Louise, tended to rationalize rather than historicize his own experience of such matters, as we know.

Of Emma, Flaubert writes: she knew that her husband would have forgiven her anything. Therefore, it would seem logical to go ask him for what little money he might have. And yet she doesn't. "The thought of Bovary's magnanimity exasperated her. . . . She would have to bear the weight of his generosity." Yet again, Emma does not preoccupy herself with hiding her misdeed because she feels some vague sense of guilt, or because she does not want to hurt her husband, or because she does not want her daughter to wind up in the gutter, but only to avoid placing herself in any position of inferiority to the man she lives with.

Casting Charles, who would certainly have understood and helped her, aside for these self-serving motives, she barely returns home before going out again to ask help of someone else. Naturally, she chooses the worst solution, one which once again demonstrates her lack of knowledge of those she has in fact lived among and loved.

Not to intimately understand the people who are near to us means betraying reality with sentiment; it means mystifying, transforming things to suit ourselves. This was one of the serious flaws that Flaubert attributed to Louise Colet. She, with her sentimentalized extravagance, heaped both praise and blame—which often were completely unfounded—upon those around her according to her impressions of the admiration, tenderness, or indifference with which they treated her, not according to any capacity whatsoever for objective observation or judgment.

Thus, exactly as Louise might have done, Emma seeks help

from the least likely person. A grain of psychological insight would have been sufficient for her to see that this is the worst possible idea. But, instead, caught up in both the urgency of her need and the memory of her ecstasy, she rushes to the house of her ex-lover, Rodolphe Boulanger. He is rich, she tells herself; he loved her; he will help her.

She finds him seated before the fire, smoking a pipe. When she enters, he is momentarily surprised, but quickly flashes a friendly smile. He still has guilt feelings to purge and also thinks she has come to speak to him of her love. Perhaps she suffers still on his account—why not smile at her?

Instinctively, Emma takes his hand, saying, "'I loved you so!'" She begins, that is, with cunning intuition to use the most basic weapons of seduction. She praises him "with coaxing little motions of the head, playful and feline," as Flaubert comments—and, actually, for once, Flaubert disappoints us with his choice of metaphor. The image of the designing, "feline" woman is conventional, unworthy of a talent as rare and sought after as his.

"'I know you love others, you may as well admit it,'" Emma goes on sweetly, "'You are a man, a real man! . . . But we'll start all over, won't we? We'll love each other as before!'" Ever the liar is Emma, ever the extortionist! Even if Rodolphe does lend her the money, how can she think she can pull off this ruse?

But, remarkably, Flaubert stops this narration of events in midstream to confess his admiration for her: "She was irresistible, with a tear trembling in her eye, like a raindrop in a blue flower-cup, after the storm."

But aren't Emma's eyes black? We enter here into the azured regions of Flaubertian eros. Could it be a memory of Louise's blue eyes that is intruding here?

Emma is, then, "irresistible." On the other hand, if she were not beautiful, how could Flaubert justify her ability to tempt a man like Rodolphe? A dead love affair returned to life, a woman who has given up everything out of sheer boredom—how could she stimulate desire in him if not through some vague inebriation of the senses that blots out the memory of the past?

Rodolphe, believing that she has returned to renew their affair, draws her to him, moved by her great tenacity, caressing with the back of his hand the two folds of black hair: "A last ray of the sun was mirrored there, like a golden arrow."

Yet, once again, it is only Emma's beauty that Flaubert cares about; he has absolutely no respect for her character, as we will see shortly, nor for Rodolphe's, if truth be told. They are two far from admirable people who are about to reveal their worst sides.

"'Why, you have been crying! Why?'" asks Rodolphe, kissing her eyelids, touched by how much she has suffered on his account. Emma breaks into sobs. He is even more flattered: "Rodolphe thought that this was an outburst of her love."

"'Oh, forgive me!'" he says to her, in an access of generosity, "'You are the only one who really pleases me. I was a fool, a wicked fool! I love you, I'll always love you! What is the matter? Tell me . . .'"

At this point, trusting his words of love, Emma passionately and sincerely confesses: "'I am ruined! You must lend me three thousand francs.'"

Rodolphe suddenly becomes very grave. All the excitement of a moment before vanishes in an instant, and his face pales. "'Ah! . . . so that's what she came for,'" he thinks, furious. His response is cool and firm: "'My dear lady, I haven't got them.'"

"A demand for money," comments Flaubert, "of all the winds that blow upon love, [is] the coldest and most destructive."

"'You haven't got them!'" Emma repeats several times, talking to herself, "'I ought to have spared myself this last shame.'" But, as always, her mortification turns immediately into combativeness: "'You never loved me,'" she presses him angrily, "'You are no better than the others.'"

"She was losing her head, giving herself away," Flaubert comments, moved by sincere pity. But Emma seems to truly enjoy "giving herself away." Not content with the reaction that her request has provoked in her ex-lover, she assails him with a vengeful and threatening speech that cannot but worsen the situation, making her seem malicious and reprehensible.

"'Oh! I feel sorry for you!'" she begins, irate: "'But when one is so poor one doesn't have silver on the butt of one's gun. One doesn't buy a clock inlaid with tortoiseshell. . . . Oh, he has all he needs! even a liqueur-stand in his bedroom; . . . you live well. You have a château, farms, woods; you go hunting; you travel to Paris. . . . Oh, I don't want anything from you; you can keep them!'"

To what lengths, one asks with bated breath, will Emma's impudence, will her foolish villainy, carry her? But now she seems unstoppable, hurtling toward the worst possible self-display.

"'But for you, and you know it, I might have lived happily,'" she shouts at him. "'There is the spot on the carpet where at my knees you swore an eternity of love. . . . Oh, your letter! your letter! it tore my heart! And then when I come back to him—to him, rich, happy, free—to implore the help the first stranger would give, a suppliant, and bringing back to him all my tenderness, he repulses me because it could cost him three thousand francs!'"

"'I haven't got them,'" he repeats impassively, "with that perfect calm with which resigned rage covers itself as with a shield." And here, notwithstanding his harsh judgment of Rodolphe, Flaubert cannot help but take his part.

Flaubert knew such "resigned rage" quite well; his letters to Louise are full to the brim of it. Perplexed, one wonders what could have motivated him to maintain for so long a relationship that caused him so much grief and "resigned rage." But why "resigned"? He was by no means forced to stay with Louise—he had not married her, nor had he ever promised her anything. What prevented him from leaving her, and why?

It might occur to some, particularly after reading the letters from the second phase of their relationship, that the meticulous Gustave still needed to keep the model of his main character before him as he wrote. And in order to do so, any rage to which he needed to resign himself would certainly have provoked a corresponding narrative fury.

This hypothesis could be defended biographically: as soon as he had finished writing *Madame Bovary*, Flaubert terminated any and all relations with Louise. Eight years of love and choler crumbled into nothingness.

But things were probably more complicated than that. Flaubert's love for Louise, at least his love for Louise's body, in all of its azured and androgynous beauty, may have so overwhelmed him that he was unable—notwithstanding his criticism and intolerance of her, and his refusal to see her more than once every two months—to break off the relationship.

Returning home after failing in her last attempt to find money, Emma stops at the pharmacy and asks for some rat poison. Homais is not in the shop at that moment, but the young shop-attendant Justin, intimidated by the woman who "seemed to him extraordinarily beautiful and majestic as a phantom," lets her take the key to the medicine closet out of his hands. Emma enters, seizes a jar, plunges her hand into it, and fills her mouth. Then she flees from the pharmacy, leaving the young man astounded and afraid.

Meanwhile, Charles has returned, by now aware of the disaster; he has looked for her everywhere and is deeply concerned for her. He will be ruined, he thinks, his name will be compromised. But what worries him most at that moment is the disappearance of his wife.

She suddenly enters, sweaty, panting, in the grip of a nervous fit that is contracting her face. "'What happened?'" Charles asks her, trying to keep her from running off. But she evades him, going to her room and closing the door after writing a brief note which she hands to him, saying, "'You are to read it to-morrow.'"

Emma has made another grave error through her impulsiveness. She thinks arsenic will cause her to die rapidly and painlessly. But this is just another of her romantic wishes. The agony will be interminable and terrible—and Flaubert cruelly compels us to watch every stage of her poisoning, without leaving out a single detail.

Other writers would probably have left off here. Not Flaubert. This forcing the reader to sit and witness all the horrifying particulars of Emma's death suggests his attitude toward realistic and naturalistic writing. But it is also a final testament to the author's repugnance for his character, comparable to an executioner's taking pleasure in his work.

When the poison begins to take effect, Emma "gently rocked her head to and fro in anguish." At the same time, she asks for something to drink because of "the frightful taste of ink" upon her tongue. Flaubert had read books and reports, had interviewed his brother the surgeon, had visited hospitals in order to research deaths resulting from poisoning. But he himself also knew the taste of ink. Taking daily doses of mercury to treat his syphilis, he often had a black tongue and the flavor of ink in his mouth.

Charles lays his hand on his wife's stomach, and she lets out a shriek. What can he do? He has yet to figure out what is causing her illness. Then her body is gripped by convulsions. Finally Charles decides to open the letter, despite her injunction to read it tomorrow. The letter says that she has swallowed poison.

When he reads that word, he begins to tremble; he tears his hair and reels throughout the room, banging into the furniture. He lacks even the strength to call out for help.

It is Félicité, the maid, who runs to call the pharmacist Homais, who in turn sends his assistant to the house of a doctor in Neufchâtel.

Bewildered and terrified, Charles is unable to make a decision. He remains kneeling next to the bed, asking his wife: "'Why did you do it? . . . Weren't you happy? Is it my fault? But I did the best I could!'"

"'Yes,'" she replies in a fading voice, caressing his head, "'you're good.'" "Of all earthly noises, Emma heard none but the intermittent lamentation of this poor heart, sweet and remote like the echo of a symphony dying away."

This word, "heart," appears everywhere in Flaubert's writing, which is curious, given his insistent refusal of all sentimentalism, all rhetoric of *Amor nel cor*. The fact is that Flaubert often views the heart merely as a piece of human anatomy, a fleshy muscle, rather than as the seat of the emotions.

"I tell you, the skin of my heart is like that of my hands, calloused," he wrote to Louise on August 31, 1846. "Give it a love bath, your poor heart, if you wish, but don't drown it" (September 2, 1846). "My heart is like a river constricted in a choked and narrow gorge; the current only flows with difficulty, always eddying and turning back on itself. It is like the Seine at Quillebeuf, full of shifting shallows. Many a vessel has been lost in it" (December 20, 1846). "This heart, in which passions, fantasies, and dreams of other worlds have been fermented in solitude, so that it is now pitted and bent like an old plate—however much you rinse it and dry it, it will always give off the cold smell of everything that has been eaten off it in the past" (January 21, 1847).

All told, there is much talk of hearts in Gustave and Louise's correspondence—but the heart of which Flaubert speaks is wasted, calloused, pocked, dulled, metallic, while Louise's is aching, swollen with tears and reproaches, with wild fits of love, and theatrical loneliness.

But we must return to Emma's interminable agonies, crucially important in Flaubert's novel. The dying Madame Bovary now sends for her daughter. The little girl arrives in the arms of her nurse. Her bare feet stick out from a nightshirt that is too short. She is set down next to her mother, and after watching her for a while says, "'Oh, how big your eyes are, mamma!'" We seem to be listening to Little Red Riding Hood at the bedside of the Big Bad Wolf. "'How pale you are! how you sweat!'" But Emma seems not to hear her daughter. She stares at Berthe to the point of frightening her, then seizes her hand to kiss it. The little girl pulls away, terrified. The mother's gaze is distant and glassy—who can tell what memories of exasperated shoves, of repeated refusals, of inexplicable impatience, may be passing through her mind at this moment?

It occurs to us to wonder: What was Flaubert's conception of the bond that unites a mother and a daughter? Did he think of it as different from the one uniting a mother and her son? And what was his idea of a mother's emotional responsibilities? Certainly, as far as his own experience was concerned, he understood quite well the feelings that linked mother and son. But what would he have said of a mother who has only a daughter?

In the novel, Emma proves to be an awful mother, not the least bit interested in the health, well-being, future, or happiness of her daughter, unable to show her anything more than a distracted and vague affection that lessens with even the slightest ill humor. What kind of mother is it, Flaubert seems to wonder, who gives her daughter, a few days after her birth, into the hands of a poor and dirty wet nurse living among flies and rats; who then raises her like a little orphan child, badly dressed and neglected; who, in a moment of anger, shoves her so hard that she falls, hurts herself, bleeds?

This was doubtlessly another of the coincidences that would have deeply offended Louise Colet when the book came out. Why detail so many aspects of Emma's behavior that anyone could easily have identified with Louise?

Emma, like Louise, is a married woman and has a daughter that she does not raise very attentively, following the old school of child rearing. In reality, Louise was very close to her daughter, but, in the eyes of the world, her bringing the child along on carriage rides with her latest lover was not exactly considered evidence of maternal inclinations. But how could Louise have explained that she lacked the funds for a nanny?

Emma is exactly like the Louise that Flaubert describes in the letters—possessive, ambitious, passionate, volatile. Emma, like Louise, exhibits great nonchalance in her manner of changing lovers, and this creates scandal.

Emma, moreover, has a weak and inept husband, just as Louise did; she was married to Hippolyte Colet, a man who knew of her affairs but did not appear offended by them.

Emma, like Louise, has an obsession with exchanging fetish objects (recall the bloody handkerchief which reappears in the novel, as well as the gloves, the slippers, the medal with the inscription *Amor nel cor*). And so, just as Gustave found this habit detestable and mannered in Louise, he likewise condemns it in Emma. At the same time, however, we know that he secretly, in the privacy of his own house, went to sniff Louise's old clothes, which he never threw out. Furthermore, the idea of keeping the bloody handkerchief and the slippers had first been his, not Louise's.

In addition, Emma, like Louise, willingly makes love in carriages, is given to making scenes, acts precipitously and unreflectively, and is egocentric and intrusive but also generous and amiable, pert and lively. She also loves to write long letters in very bad taste (or, at least, letters that Flaubert judged to be in bad taste, as he did those of Victor Hugo and Lamartine).

It would not have been difficult for Flaubert's contemporaries to recognize in the blundering adulteress Emma the poetess with the checkered romantic life who had been Flaubert's lover for fully five years.

Yes, it is true, Emma has black hair and Louise was blonde. Emma wears hers separated into two bands that cover her ears, while Louise wore ringlets that cascaded around her cheeks. And Emma's eyes are black while Louise's were blue (and yet Flaubert errs not once but twice in calling Emma's eyes blue—a very odd slip for an author so meticulous and precise).

If he wanted to make the model for his character unrecognizable, why did he leave so many overt traces that lead one to the person of Louise?

It is certain, as Maxime Du Camp said, that for the plot of *Madame Bovary* Flaubert was inspired by a contemporary event, the famous suicide of Madame Delamare, well-known adulteress, which the newspapers had reported at great length. It is probable that for certain details of Emma's affairs, Flaubert was inspired by the diaries of Ludovica Louise d'Arcet Pradier. But it is likewise certain that we find much of Louise Colet's character as well as behavior in Emma.

Flaubert, however, felt that merely depicting in one's works, however covertly, someone that one knew, was insufficiently creative and overly personal. And he reproached Louise for not being able to "refrain" from doing so herself.

He lectured her on the subject and intimidatingly discouraged her from publishing a play in which the philosopher Victor Cousin, one of her former lovers, is too easily recognized as one of the characters: "Since you have to read your play to the Académie Française, I want to tell you practically what I think of it. The Philosopher [Cousin], underneath his extremely transparent mask, is clearly a satiric portrait; that name ending in 'in' [the character's name is Dherbin] would be enough to make him recognizable to everyone; he himself will perceive it, and will harbor an eternal rancor toward you. You do a disservice to Henriette, and to yourself most of all. . . . Minimize, therefore, the similarities between Dherbin and the Philosopher. Make him into a legitimist, or whatever you like, rather than a doctrinaire, etcetera. Think about it; I think this advice is important for your life, for your career" (May 2, 1852).

Louise was extremely bitter after the publication of *Madame Bovary*. Unlike many of Flaubert's other works, which she had read and reread before they came out, this one caught her by surprise, with all the unpleasantness of a bucketful of ice water in the face. But she could not openly express her displeasure, since that would have amounted to a tacit admission that she had served as the model for Emma and would only have increased the damage to her.

As a result, Louise limited herself to tracing out a quite vague and imprecise portrait of Flaubert, buried in a novel primarily about the love affairs of George Sand and Alfred de Musset, including Musset's courtship of Louise herself.

"I want to cover those two years with a black crepe like those used by patrician families in Venice to cover portraits of relatives condemned to death," Louise wrote, speaking of Flaubert, in her novel *Lui*, which was published in 1864:

> I had seen the proud and arrogant recluse deny all his doctrines on art and love one by one and sell his opinions for small change — and for his least lofty lusts.
>
> When conscience no longer guides our actions, when self-interest and vanity become the spirit's sole motives, then any notion of honor and idealism disappears. . . . From thence, unrecognized traitors, cruel voluptuaries who hide their murderous instincts behind a smile, agitators of human affairs, ready for any crime, are decorated in public with the title of statesmen.[12]

Elsewhere she had spoken of *Madame Bovary* as "the novel of a traveling salesman."

Flaubert in turn commented to his friend Ernest Feydeau: "Do you want to have a little fun? Do me (or rather do yourself) the favor of buying *Lui*, Mme Louise Colet's current novel. You will recognize your friend, who is soundly thrashed in it. . . . You cannot possibly imagine such baseness. . . . I come out of it as white as snow, but as a man unfeeling, greedy, truly a dim-witted imbecile. This is what comes of having copulated with Muses. I laughed until my sides were splitting. . . . What a ridiculous thing, to put literature at the service of the passions in this way, and what pathetic works it makes for, in every possible sense" (November 12, 1859).

Actually, the novel *Lui* is not at all bad, nor is it vulgar. If anything, it is simply boring and wordy, all prattle and threadbare romance, verbally clumsy and opaque. But both de Musset and Flaubert are treated with great delicacy and some tenderness. Not to mention the central character, Antonia Back, a famous woman

---

12. Louise Colet, *"Lui": A View of Him*, trans. Marilyn Gaddis Rose (Athens, Ga.: University of Georgia Press, 1986), 312–13.

writer (George Sand), who is painted as a woman of great talent and iron will, who possesses a profound sense of irony.

Flaubert, however, did everything to discredit his ex-inamorata: "My affair with Mme Colet," he wrote in November of 1859 to Amélie Bousquet, "left me no 'wound,' in the sentimental and deep sense of that word; what remains is a memory (and even now a sensation) of a very long irritation. Her book was the culminating blow."

Flaubert was without question a great artist; Louise Colet was not. But he, not she, was the first to denigrate the ex-lover in writing—with no compunction, we might add, about "putting literature at the service of the passions." What she wrote about him in her very moderate novel is quite a small matter compared to the grotesque monument to her in *Madame Bovary*.

A brief examination of the dates in no way amends the conclusions we can draw about how the great novelist utilized the living model for his novel's main character.

Flaubert and Louise Colet met in 1846. After the first enthusiastic months, Flaubert began to write increasingly evasive, and sometimes downright offensive, letters. This does not mean, however, that he stopped seeing her, though he saw her more and more rarely and always hurriedly. The correspondence, on the other hand, became increasingly abundant. Louise, exactly like Emma, had asked for a letter a day. And he, after demurring a bit, acquiesced.

On August 21, 1848, Gustave wrote Louise a laconic little letter that consisted of only these words: "Thank you for the gift. Thank you for your nice verses. Thank you for your good wishes." And that's it. The relationship was over after two years of furtive encounters and hundreds of letters. He left for the Orient with Maxime Du Camp.

On July 26, 1851, returning from a trip, Flaubert sent Louise a letter: "I write you because 'my heart prompts me to speak kindly to you,' dear friend. If I could make you happy I should joyfully do so; it would be only fair. I feel guilty at the thought of having made you suffer so; don't you understand that? However, neither I, nor you, but only the circumstances, can be held responsible for this—and for all the rest."

On September 19, 1851, Flaubert began to write *Madame Bovary*. Could it be that those "words from the heart" were not perfectly disinterested? We know that Flaubert liked to work the way painters do, with his model before him. And he was precise and exacting in his observations and note-taking. He relates how on several occasions he went in person to gather information on various details of the novel: the ball, the agricultural fair, the castle, the various ways of performing surgery on clubfeet: "I am still struggling with clubfeet. My dear brother failed to keep two appointments with me this week, and unless he comes tomorrow I shall be forced to make another trip to Rouen" (April 22, 1854). He wrote to Louise Colet: "How many fierce dramas I imagined at the morgue, where I was determined to go" (July 7, 1853). "This morning I was at an agricultural fair, and I returned home exhausted and bored to death" (July 18, 1852). To Louis Bouilhet he wrote that he needed "the scientific words that describe the different parts of the eye" (September 19, 1855). "I have to go to Rouen to get information on arsenic poisonings" (October 5, 1855).

On March 6, 1855, Flaubert wrote a last letter to Louise Colet, after a correspondence of three years during which he continually called her "poor heart," "my poor heart," and the like, as if he wanted to make her aware of the poverty of his love but at the same time call her attention to her function in the plot of his novel.

On October 1, Flaubert published the first episode of *Madame Bovary* in the magazine *La Revue de Paris*, edited by Maxime Du Camp. Louise, who had not been allowed to read a single line of the manuscript, which Flaubert instead read aloud to other more or less intimate friends, saw it in print only after all relations with the "master" had been harshly severed, according to his will.

"It is my understanding that yesterday evening you took pains, three times, to come to see me. I was not at home. And in fear of the kinds of reactions that such insistence on your part could elicit on my part, the rules of *savoir vivre* constrain me to advise you: I will never be at home for you. I have the honor of saluting you. G. F." (March 6, 1855).

❧❧❧

There are still several things that remain to be said about the mother-daughter relationship as Flaubert depicts it, a relationship that foreshadows the one, much more important for Flaubert, between mother and son.

Emma Bovary, as far as the author is concerned, is undoubtedly a bad mother. In order to demonstrate this, Flaubert constructs very specific scenes, which follow a very formulaic narrative pattern: from Emma's first rejection of her daughter, upon learning at her birth that the baby is a girl, to her consigning the infant child to the hands of a wet nurse living in want in a filthy hovel; from the time that the baby spits up on her mother and she hands it away with annoyance, to when, just afterward, she leaves the house of the wet nurse—who is pestering her for more money for the baby's care—with an impatient and disgusted "'All right, all right!'"

The baby grows up having received fatherly, but not motherly, affection. When she can still only hold herself up on her weak little legs with great difficulty, we are present at the painful scene when she is pushed and, tumbling against the bureau handle, cuts her cheek. Then, watching her child while she sleeps, after the baby's father has treated her injured face, all smeared with dried tears and blood, her mother thinks, "'how ugly this child is!'"

On a page of Louise Colet's diary from 1842, we find a notation about her daughter that greatly resembles this scene from the novel. Louise, while watching her sleeping daughter, observes: "My daughter's character fills me with pain; she has the envious and trifling spirit of her father."[13]

Since Louise was in the habit of reading her diary to Flaubert, it could not be more likely that she read the *mémento* about her daughter to the "master." It is equally likely that he transferred it to his novel, transforming the moral comment into an aesthetic one. This would have been perfectly consistent with his character.

At the end, we find Emma, on her deathbed, looking at her daughter with a gaze so glassy and delirious that it frightens the little girl. "'Oh, how big your eyes are, mamma!'" The better to see

13. Colet, quoted in *Rage and Fire*, 169.

121

you with, my dear! In those eyes, there is certainly neither affection nor regret at having to leave her child.

In his letters to Louise, in fact, Gustave's judgment of how she raised her child never appears. Flaubert proved to be extremely discreet about this complex and intimate relationship. And yet, from the odd and indirect hints that he made, we understand that he did not favorably view his lover's way of being a mother. This is not because Louise did not show affection to her little girl: she continually covered her with kisses and brought her everywhere. What bothered him was precisely that in doing so, Louise made the little girl a witness to her affairs.

This, however, was Louise's nature; she kept no secrets from anyone, least of all from her daughter. The appeal of her artless and impetuous character derived from this trait. She felt a kind of elation at airing her "dirty laundry"—her affections, jealousies, anguish, worries.

Aloof and guarded men like the philosopher Victor Cousin and Gustave Flaubert were undoubtedly pained by Louise's compulsive self-revelation, even as they were attracted to precisely those elements of her exuberant and extravagant character.

Louise, moreover, as her diaries indicate, was never quite sure that her husband was her daughter's father, even if she often found his traits in her. For years the philosopher Cousin believed the little girl to be his, even if Louise had never said so definitively. "I know, you never said with certainty that Henriette is my daughter . . ."

This indicates that Louise never sacrificed her honesty, even when it might have been advantageous to do so. In truth, she probably did not even know herself which man was Henriette's father, especially at the beginning of the child's life. But by the time the little girl had become an adolescent, Louise found in her the unmistakable characteristics of her husband's weakness. Notwithstanding all of the ambiguity as to who sired her, Victor Cousin grew so fond of Henriette that he left her a small inheritance after his death. Such a fact reveals a remarkable broad-mindedness on his part, when we consider the prejudices of the age.

The funny thing is that often, in his letters to Louise, Flaubert urged her to marry the old philosopher. The two lovers could still continue to see each other. But, in the meantime, she should see that she is taken care of, for the well-being of her daughter!

Years later, it was Cousin who urged Louise to marry Flaubert, "for your well-being" and "for the well-being of the baby." But met with her timid suggestions that they be married, Flaubert categorically refused; he is not free, already has enormous family responsibilities, and cannot do it.

In the midst of all these uncertainties, Louise wrote an extremely tender poem about her daughter:

> Having you ever with me is my sweetest dream
> the house is filled with the sound of your footsteps
> and when you sleep at night I get up
> to watch you sleep in your tiny bed.
> On the pillow rests your tender neck
> the turned-down sheet reveals your small round arm
> your face smiles upon the white linen
> your golden hair caresses your forehead.

From a literary point of view, the poem is certainly entirely conventional. But we feel that it is sincere, and the love for her daughter real. Good poems, however, are not made of sincerity only.

> I place a flower on your angelic head
> you dance, you laugh, we go to the ball
> And I am happy at every glance
> that your virginal manner attracts as you pass.

For Flaubert, inferior literature could not be detached from inferior sentiments. Too harsh? He never wrote anything about his mother, perhaps because he feared losing control of his style. Theirs was undoubtedly a complicated, thorny relationship, not without its reciprocal bullying and torments.

"My mother was waiting for me at the station," Flaubert wrote to Louise, after his first encounter with her, which kept him away from Croisset for three days. "She wept at seeing me return. You wept at seeing me leave. In other words, such is our woe that we cannot move a league without causing tears on two sides at once!" (August 4, 1846).

And also: "Yesterday, and the day before, my mother was in a frightful state." This was the period in which Gustave took whatever opportunity he could to see Louise. "She had delusions of death. I stayed beside her."

"You always speak to me of your pain," Flaubert wrote to Louise on August 23, 1846, "But I have seen another pain. A pain that is here, near me, and that never complains, that even smiles, and compared to which your pain, however excessive it may be, will never be but as a puncture likened to a burn, as a spasm placed side by side with death pangs. And these are the straits that I find myself in: the two women whom I love the most have my heart fastened in a harness with two bridles and are stretching it. I am being pulled back and forth between love and anguish."

At Louise's protests that a man cannot spend his whole life with his mother, Flaubert coolly replied: "My life is tethered to another's, and such will be the case as long as that other exists. Seaweed that is tossed by the waves, I am held to the rock by a single tough strand. . . . If the strand were severed, where would the poor useless plant tumble?" (August 27 or 28, 1846).

Louise responded by accusing him of hiding behind his mother's skirts "like a virgin." "You believed you could wound my vanity," he calmly replied, "saying that I am chaperoned like an unmarried girl. Five or six years ago, I would have done something crazy, would have had myself killed in order to blot out the effect of such words on me; today they run off me like water from the neck of a swan. Do you not think that it would be delightful for me, for me alone, being the man that I am, to have you here? What could I possibly be risking? Nothing, absolutely nothing. My mother, even if she knew, would not say a word about it; I know her. She might be jealous of you (when your daughter is eighteen, you will understand that one can be jealous of one's own daughter, and you will hate her husband: that is the rule). But that is all" (September 5, 1846).

With these words, Flaubert confirms Louise's accusation: he himself compares himself to a marriageable girl of eighteen, while he is twenty-five and is not expecting to get married.

"It is for your name, for your honor, to not see you sullied by the stupid jokes of the first who comes along, to save you from blushing before the customs officers who stroll along the walls, so that a domestic does not laugh in your face. But you don't understand. No, not at all," Flaubert wrote in the same letter of September 5. But then we discover from other letters that it is not true that Flaubert was worried about her. And it is not even true that his mother was not jealous or, at least, that he was not afraid of provoking his mother's jealousy. He was terribly afraid.

"I made up a little story that my mother believed, but the poor woman was extremely anxious all day yesterday. She came to the station at eleven and spent the whole night without sleeping, tormenting herself with worry. This morning I found her on the platform in a state of extreme anxiety. She did not reproach me once, but her expression was the greatest reproach of all" (September 10, 1846). All this because her son Gustave had spent the night in Mantes with his lover!

"Yesterday my mother was in my room while I was doing my toilet. . . . They bring me a letter. She takes it, inspects the handwriting, and says, in a half-joking manner: 'I would really like to know what is in here.' I responded with a silly laugh that I tried to make sound comic, so as to remove any serious doubt from her mind. I don't know if she suspects anything. Maybe so. The regularity of the postman is quite marvelous" (September 13, 1846).

And yet, it is precisely that "marvelous postman" who was an involuntary accomplice in a subterfuge that, as we have seen, lasted for years: so as not to arouse suspicions in his mother, Gustave required Louise to address her letters to Maxime Du Camp, who then sent them in a new envelope to Croisset as if he were the one who had originally posted them.

"Never come here," Gustave enjoined Louise, "Here it would be impossible, topographically speaking, to meet. I well know that the idea of the encounter itself is not what inspires you, but it is after all still a more than merely incidental appetizer, and inevitably serves to fortify all the banquets of the heart. It would be better for you to stay in Rouen. You could come in the morning, having informed me the day before. I could make up some errand as a pretext and then be back here again around six" (September 14, 1846).

And to Louise's insistent questions about when they would be able to leave together, Flaubert responded: "Ah, if we were free, we would travel together! It is a dream I often have" (September 17, 1846).

Flaubert was speaking of a purely theoretical desire, of course, since as far as trips were concerned, he planned and took many—within France as well as to England, to Africa as well as Asia—but never felt the need to invite Louise, not once.

"My mother needs me," was his most frequent answer, even if only to a request that they go to Paris. "Even my most brief absence does her ill. Her pain imposes a thousand unimaginable constraints upon me. What for others would be as nothing, for me is a lot. I am not able to say 'Get lost!' to those who beg me with sad looks and tears in their eyes" (September 30, 1846).

But Louise had begged him many times, "with sad looks and tears in [her] eyes," to come to see her or to meet her elsewhere, and he was easily able to tell *her* to "get lost."

"I am as weak as a baby, and I give in because I cannot stand the reproaches, the pleading, the sighs. For example, last year I went sailing every day. I ran no risk since, in addition to my nautical abilities, I am a rather good swimmer. Nevertheless, this year my mother took it into her head to become afraid for me. She did not tell me to quit this sport, which for me, with the strong tides we are having now, is full of excitement: I cut across the wave that drenches me as it leaps over the sides of the boat; I let the wind swell the sail that quivers and snaps with lively motions; I am alone, without words, without thought, given over completely to the forces of nature, and I relish the feeling of being dominated by it. My mother, as I say, said nothing about any of this: nevertheless, I put all of my equipment in the attic, and not a day goes by that I am not seized by the desire to take it down again. But I do nothing so as to avoid certain remarks, certain looks; that is why. It is for the same reason that for ten years I kept secret the fact that I wrote, so I could save myself any potential ridicule" (September 30, 1846).

Flaubert does not say that his mother feared he might have an epileptic seizure out on the water. This wordless maternal oppression, made up of looks, repressed tears, oblique comments, and silent agreements, is curious. It is still more curious that young

Gustave, in his clandestine flight from such a domination, sought out another, however different, one.

"I would need to find some pretext for going to Paris, but what? I would need to find another for the second trip and so on and so forth. Not having anyone but me to keep her attached to life, my mother spends her days pondering all the possible misfortunes and accidents that could befall me" (September 30, 1846).

"This evening I was able to flee only with great difficulty. My mother is sick, and I made my escape under the pretext of spending a half hour with Maxime" (November 29, 1846).

Don't these subterfuges resemble those of certain philandering husbands who attempt to mislead their jealous and suspicious wives, from whom they want to keep the existence of a new mistress hidden?

The relationship between mother and son in the Flaubert household was neither among the most simple nor the most transparent, made up as it was of continuous petty blackmails, pathetic fibs, subtle jealousies, sublime renunciations, and mistreatment, fear, and buried intolerance. And yet, in many letters it seems that Flaubert blames Louise, and Emma even more, for not being like his mother, the incredibly heroic Anne Justine Caroline Flériot, later Madame Flaubert.

Both Madame Bovary and Madame Colet are mothers unable to be patient and supportive, to silently smile, to get their way without blaming others, to give of themselves without asking anything in return. It is as if a compliant and tyrannical motherhood, simultaneously forlorn and possessive, meek and vengeful, were the only possibility, the sole form of maternity that could earn the "eternal" love of a son.

And what of fatherhood? What place did Flaubert give it in the family? In all of Flaubert's stories, mothers are more often present, stronger and more decisive than fathers. Fathers either behave like perennial children or keep out of the way and watch, not daring to intervene.

The young Flaubert was certainly terrified of fatherhood. It was one of the things that frightened him the most about his relationship with Louise. Consequently, it is odd that in *Madame*

Bovary there is not a single mention of the pregnancies Emma would have tried to avoid in her affairs.

How many times Gustave asked Louise if "the English had arrived" (since the English soldiers wore red coats)! The metaphor is quite dainty, and Flaubert used it often. "I won't pretend that your letter announcing the arrival of the English did not cause me great joy. May the god of coitus ensure that I never again have to endure such anxiety. I don't know how I didn't fall sick, as they say. My blood ran cold as I awaited yours" (December 7, 1852).

And when Louise mentioned with trepidation the possibility of having a child with him, he quickly wrote back: "The idea of causing the birth of someone horrifies me. I should curse myself were I to become a father. I, have a son! Oh, no! No! No! I desire my flesh to perish, and have no wish to transmit to anyone the troubles and ignominies of existence. . . . Every principle of my being would be repelled by such a possibility, and yet, and yet . . . " (December 11, 1852).

Flaubert's anxiety about fatherhood went beyond the practical considerations of a man who lives alone, who does not have much money, who wants to dedicate himself to his work, and who possesses no desire to have a family of his own. His was a fear that greatly surpassed such reasonable concerns. It was as if, in that house in Croisset, the generative principle had been enacted once and for all, creating a situation that could not have been disrupted without the most serious of consequences. A mother is a mother always, and a son always a son. Becoming a father in his turn, the son would shift the direction of affections, destroying a delicate and precious equilibrium, and would enter the domain of the unnatural and the catastrophic.

But, upon further consideration, we also find in Flaubert an aversion to himself, a profound and visceral disdain that is the other face of his infantile fantasy of omnipotence.

The grand depiction of Emma Bovary's death throes is not yet over. The famous Dr. Canivet enters the room of the dying woman. The first thing he does is prescribe a strong emetic. And miserable, unfortunate Emma, already half-dead, is now forced to vomit up her guts. "Her limbs were convulsed, her whole body covered with brown spots, and her pulse slipped beneath the fingers like a stretched thread, like a harp-string about to break."

At this point, Emma begins "to scream horribly." She curses the poison and begs it to accomplish its work quickly, "thrust[ing] away with her stiffened arms everything that Charles, in more agony than herself, tried to make her drink."

In the meanwhile, another doctor arrives, the prestigious Dr. Larivière, who enters to the reverent bowing of Homais. The doctor determines at a glance that by now the poison has had its effect and that there is nothing more to be done. "*Du courage!*" he says, turning to Charles, exactly as Rodolphe had said to Emma when he cravenly abandoned her on the day they had planned to flee together.

"*Du courage!*" was also all that Maxime Du Camp wrote to Louise Colet to console her when Gustave decided to leave for the Orient without her.

After having consoled poor Charles a bit, the great luminary directs his steps toward Homais's house. The latter, "who could not by temperament keep away from celebrities," has prepared a succulent repast, sending out to the Lion d'Or for the dishes.

And so, while in a nearby house the dying Emma suffers horribly, in the Homais home the great professor Larivière gorges himself on cutlets and pigeon.

Sartre suggests that the description of Professor Larivière is in reality a portrait of Flaubert's father, the celebrated, esteemed, and honored Achille-Cléophas Flaubert, who had wanted to force his son to study law; in order to avoid such a fate, the child had to "choose" a terrible illness, epilepsy.

In Emma's house, meanwhile, the spectacle of death continues. Flaubert has no intention whatsoever of ending the matter so quickly. One is reminded of certain concerts of the music of unknown composers, when one thinks, "Here we are at the end," because of a decisive turn the music has taken—the woodwinds plunging, the rhythms of the cymbals quickening, the melody's air of finality—and, just as we get ready to clap our hands, the tension fades suddenly, and the music recommences with its pianissimos, crescendos, andantes, and adagios.

On her deathbed, Emma "had her eyes inordinately wide open, and her poor hands wandered over the sheets with that hideous and gentle movement of the dying, that seems as if they already wanted to cover themselves with the shroud."

Finally, the priest—called by whom, we do not know—appears to deliver extreme unction. This is the moment at which Flaubert's gaze scans for the last time the body of his heroine, now lying supine: the priest "dipped his right thumb in the oil, and began to give extreme unction. First, upon the eyes, that had so coveted all worldly goods; then upon the nostrils, that had been so greedy of the warm breeze and the scents of love; then upon the mouth, that had spoken lies, moaned in pride and cried out in lust; then upon the hands, that had taken delight in the texture of sensuality; and finally upon the soles of the feet, so swift when she had hastened to satisfy her desires, and that would now walk no more."

This scene was one of the ones most targeted by the censors, who accused it of desecrating a thing as pious and holy as extreme unction. It is indeed a cruel moment, but not blasphemous. If anything, it conjures up the image of a still living body in the throes of death, even the image of a murder in progress. This could be the homicide of a character by her author, performed with the desperate joy of an ancient vendetta, profound and lacerating—so lacerating, it gives the impression that the author has also slain a part of himself, perhaps the part that, when all is said and done, mattered most to him, even if he in no way loved it.

Flaubert, a year or two previously, in August 1847, had been struck by an event that all the newspapers had reported: the duke of Praslin had murdered his wife. A week later he committed suicide by taking arsenic.

That September, Louise had sent Flaubert the letters of the duchess of Praslin, which had been published in a newspaper.

Flaubert replied: "I will read the letters of Madame de Praslin. The little that I know about the affair seems strange to me. One thing struck me: it is that these letters reminded me, at moments, of the flavor of yours. You will laugh, but this parallel, however crazy it may be, leaped out before my eyes because of its very truth. We must hope the parallel will go no further, and that I will never murder you. But who knows? No matter, it would be funny" (September 17, 1847).

We know that Louise wrote to him about jumping from the carriage to escape de Musset's assault. Had not Flaubert then imagined her dead in the street, her head crushed by the horses' hooves?

Who knows whether the death of Emma Bovary did not in some way constitute the achievement of that crime that had so lingered in the imagination of Gustave Flaubert.

I n Emma's room, death has not yet decided to shut her eyes.
Madame Bovary's face, writes Flaubert, "had an expression of
serenity as if the sacrament had cured her." Charles begins to
think that maybe she will pull through after all.

As if confirming his hope, Emma now weakly asks for a mirror. When she has it in her hands, she remains bent over it, perplexed, bewitched. In the next moment, large tears fall and stain
the smooth surface of the glass. "Then she turned away her head
with a sigh and fell back upon the pillows."

This seems to be the end. But it is only another false finale.
Flaubert's gaze will not leave Emma's dying body; he will not do
her the courtesy of letting her draw her last breath in peace.

We are immediately informed that her breathing has gotten
heavy, that "the whole of her tongue protruded from her mouth,"
that her rolling eyes "grew paler, like the two globes of a lamp that
is going out," that as her "death-rattle became stronger the priest
prayed faster; his prayer mingled with Bovary's stifled sobs."

Suddenly, a clattering of wooden shoes coming down the street,
accompanied by the rhythmic tapping of a cane, drowns out all
other sounds. A voice rings out, a "raucous voice," singing, "*Sou-
vent la chaleur d'un beau jour* . . ."[14]

Emma rises up "like a galvanised corpse; her hair streaming,
her eyes fixed, staring."

It is the blind man, whose song Emma has heard before, during the course of her adultery, with a shiver of fear. And now, at
the very end, the blind man appears at Emma's bedside as if she
had an appointment with horror. She who has so loved handsome
men is visited at the brink of death by a bloody, mocking mask of
masculinity.

"'The blind man!'" she cries, "and she began to laugh, an atrocious, frantic, desperate laugh, thinking she saw the hideous face of
the poor wretch loom out of the eternal darkness like a menace."

"A final spasm threw her back upon the mattress. They all drew
near. She had ceased to exist."

14. In de Man's translation, this line and the one following it read:

Often the heat of a summer's day
Makes a young girl dream her heart away.

This scene of the blind man is clearly out of tune with the rest of the book, devoid of the story's limpid conciseness, lacking the soberness of the narrative rhythm. It is an added bit of exasperated romanticism, a little touch of "poor taste" of the kind for which Flaubert would have acerbically reproached Louise, the falsifying intrusion of rhetoric upon events, of symbol upon object. A descent into the vulgarity of a too insistent, redundant, and emblematic punishment.

The reader, however, breathes a sigh of relief. The spectacle of Emma's death scene has finally reached a conclusion. Now, we hope, we have finally left behind all the ghastly details.

But the author does not see things this way. He wants to square accounts with what is left of Madame Bovary, with her lifeless body, still enveloped in the mystique of her beauty, the bewitching and perverse vision demanding that havoc be wrought upon it to its utmost degree.

Emma is then dressed in her bridal gown—in white—according to Charles's wishes, notwithstanding the protests of Homais, who thinks this idea "'excessive.'" But for once Charles imposes his will. He will not only dress his dead wife in bridal clothes but will put on her the elegant slippers she received from the Marquis of Andervilliers, as well as a coronet of flowers. The fetish objects will be buried with the body of the beloved.

Madame Lefrançois and Mother Bovary approach the dead woman to dress her. "'Look at her. . . . How pretty she still is! Now, couldn't you swear she was going to get up in a minute?'"

Madame Lefrançois bends over the body of the young woman to raise her head. But as she lifts her up, "a rush of black liquid poured from her mouth, as if she were vomiting."

A taste for the revolting comes over our author in this scene. The dead Emma, who still seems so fresh that she could get out of bed any minute, must be represented to us in all of the monstrosity of her corrupted flesh. Do you see what will happen to those who prefer the pleasures of the senses to modesty and chasteness? There is something in this scene meant to frighten every restless wife, unhappy with her husband, into whose hands this book falls. This is precisely the argument that, at the famous censorship trial of *Madame Bovary*, the defense will make.

133

In the meanwhile, relatives and friends arrive for the wake. They begin to discuss religion, politics, all the while eating and drinking, and then they fall heavily asleep.

Only Charles remains awake. He comes on tiptoe into the stifling room and approaches the body of his wife, which irresistibly attracts him. The candle wax falls "in great drops upon the sheets of the bed."

With two fingers, Charles delicately raises her veil, then lets out a scream of horror. Emma no longer looks as tranquil, as reposed, as when he had last seen her. Her face bears the stamp of her horrible death, and of the final demonic laugh that convulsed her before her heart seized.

"The corner of her mouth, which was open, seemed like a black hole at the lower part of her face; . . . a kind of white dust besprinkled her lashes, and her eyes were beginning to disappear in a viscous pallor, as if covered by a spiderweb."

Dr. Bovary, beside himself, is led away from her body by his sympathetic friends. But he returns a second time and cries that he will allow her to be put in the coffin only if a lock of her hair is cut off for him to save as a remembrance.

The servant girl, Félicité, armed with a pair of scissors, approaches the body of her mistress but dares not touch her, overwhelmed as she is by unbearable sadness and pain. So Homais takes the scissors from the girl and strides toward the corpse.

But "he trembled so that he nicked the skin of the temple in several places. At last, stiffening himself against emotion, Homais gave two or three great cuts at random that left white patches amongst that beautiful black hair."

Here, with this scene, we witness the final assault upon Emma's body, brutalized, ravaged by poison, contorted by death, bloody, with a hole for a mouth, her temples punctured with scissors, her hair cut off in ragged clumps, and her eyes covered by a whitish "spiderweb."

The novel continues for two more chapters, which concern the "post-Emma" period. We also note that the novel's tone will become once again gentle and poetic, lovely, the drive to fully enact the adulteress's exemplary punishment having exhausted itself.

Charles finds himself at the mercy of his creditors, reduced to poverty, in a house without furniture or food, alone with little Berthe, who is dressed in rags.

We first met Dr. Bovary when he was just a boy, as he entered a classroom of smart alecks and became the butt of their jokes. We remember his gawkiness, represented by his cap, which was simultaneously unique and common: "It was one of those head-gears of composite order, in which we can find traces of the bear- and the coonskin, the shako, the bowler, and the cotton nightcap; one of those poor things, in fine, whose dumb ugliness has depths of expression, like an imbecile's face."

But we now see Charles in his maturity, near to a death which he himself will also seek, but in a more gentle manner, just as his life had been gentle and humble.

Is it not possible that the commonness everyone accuses Charles of is only an expression of the dogged, backward faithful-ness proper to a man whose character is lazy, kind, timorous, and peace-loving?

His love for his wife seems to be the one thing that Flaubert is least able to criticize. We are a long way from being able to infer from this, however, that Flaubert wants us to love Charles as a character. And yet there is something in Charles that Flaubert is not able to make into a joke. I am speaking of his ability, truly rare, to love without asking anything in return. This love is not a capit-ulation, as Emma believes, but virtually a religious passion.

Nevertheless, at this point we might ask ourselves again: What exactly is the nature of the relationship between Flaubert and Charles Bovary? Perhaps only one word serves to define it: ambiguity.

On the one hand, favoring the opinions of Charles's contem-poraries, citizens of Yonville and Rouen, Flaubert represents him as a dullard, a shabby and uncouth individual who because of his simplemindedness deserves to be betrayed, a provincial numskull, in a word, with no hope of redemption.

But, on the other hand, there is a certain tolerance in Flaubert, layered with secret sympathy, for the "simple heart" of Charles. (Let us remember that "A Simple Heart" is the title of one of Flaubert's most beautiful stories; it is the elegant, spare, and def-erential portrait of the servant girl who attended and loved him for years. It is almost as if a part of this author's character had submerged itself in such simplicity—a part, however, to be ashamed of and to dream over.)

To understand Flaubert's ambiguity toward Charles, we need only follow him through the last two chapters of the novel, our attention no longer distracted by the obtrusive and egocentric protagonist, Emma Bovary. When she is on stage, it is difficult to notice anyone else.

The author, with exhausted and indulgent gaze, now follows Charles's daydreams. And, for once, he does not disparage them since, however abstract (like Emma's) they may be, they have the great virtue of not being inspired by literature.

While Homais becomes increasingly more vulgar, every day growing more overbearing and arrogant, more vain and presumptuous, Charles Bovary, in the way he slips into solitude and sadness, evokes something that we might call a "tentative tenderness" on the part of the author and, hence, of the reader.

Not even little Berthe, who will wind up abandoned and penniless, gets more than conventional pity from Flaubert. She will be orphaned by both mother and father, will end up first at her grandmother's, then, after her grandmother's death, with an aunt who, unable to support her, will send her off to labor as a millworker. But this social "descent" is just barely suggested and in no way dramatized.

In contrast, the events which befall Charles Bovary in his last months are reported with emotion and sympathy. Charles dies, literally, of love, holding a lock of his wife's hair, after having read with intense and anxious attention the letters written to Emma by Léon and Rodolphe.

He had met Rodolphe shortly after Emma's death, in the market at Argueil, where Charles had come to sell his mare, the last of his possessions.

"They both turned pale when they caught sight of one another. Rodolphe, who had only sent his card for the funeral, first stammered some apologies, then grew bolder, and even invited Charles (it was in the month of August and very hot) to share a bottle of beer with him at the terrace of a café."

Charles, a meek and timid soul, lacks the courage to refuse.

However, this is not exclusively out of weakness but from a polite desire not to offend him by refusing.

"Leaning his elbows on the table, [Rodolphe] chewed his cigar as he talked, and Charles was lost in reverie at the sight of the face she had loved. He seemed to find back something of her there. It was quite a shock to him. He would have liked to have been this man."

How profound Flaubert's intuition is here, how deftly he is able to cast off the spell of the mundane laws of psychology to say the unsayable. A man, even an intensely loving man, who does not know jealousy is either heartless or a fool, the citizens of Rouen — and of today — would have said.

And yet Charles Bovary, the awkward man, the man beaten, betrayed, made a fool of, incapable of anything but the pure act of loving, arrives by a lover's instinct at something much more sophisticated and modern: respect for the other in and for himself, out of a pure desire for reality.

To desire that one's beloved remain her- or himself, with all defects and peculiarities intact, even if they cause the lover pain, to not aspire to change the other but to accept that person with all her or his deformities, beyond all traditional codes of possessiveness: these are things that belong to an imagined world of the future. Rodolphe "went on talking of agriculture, cattle and fertilizers, filling with banalities all the gaps where an allusion might slip in. Charles was not listening to him; Rodolphe noticed it, and he could follow the sequence of memories that crossed his face. This face gradually reddened; Charles's nostrils fluttered, his lips quivered. For a moment, Charles stared at him in somber fury and Rodolphe, startled and terrified, stopped talking. But soon the same look of mournful weariness returned to his face."

"'I can't blame you for it,'" Charles says to him. Rodolphe remains silent. How dare this man raise an issue that he is doing everything he can to avoid? "'No, I can't blame you any longer,'" Charles continues, perfectly calm, "'Fate willed it this way.'"

Rodolphe, "who had been the agent of this fate," Flaubert pointedly remarks, "thought him very meek for a man in his situation, comic even and slightly despicable."

One feels the author's tremendous resistance to being seduced into feelings of pity for the defeated, cowardly, bereft character. He seems on the verge of approving Rodolphe's opinion—even though Rodolphe, on the score of cowardice and weakness, is much more contemptible than poor Charles. The haughty judgment of his friends, the power of group belief, could never forgive Flaubert's yielding before the placid humility of the vanquished.

Flaubert's finer empathy goes to Charles Bovary, but secretly, to ensure that no one finds out, God forbid, that Flaubert isn't "dissolute and rebellious, subversive and skeptical" enough.

The next morning, Charles goes to sit on the bench in the back of the garden, where Emma and her lover kissed while he slept. "Rays of light were straying through the trellis, the vine leaves threw their shadows on the sand, jasmines perfumed the blue air[,] . . . and Charles was panting like an adolescent under the vague desires of love that filled his aching heart."

> At seven o'clock little Berthe who had not seen him all afternoon, came to fetch him for dinner. . . . "Papa, come!"
> And thinking he wanted to play, she gave him a gentle push. He fell to the ground. He was dead.

Such is the death of a man who never really tested his luck, who chose to love a person who could not help but hurt him. A lover of pain? A masochist? No, because what is at stake here does not concern a search for pleasure within pain but rather, if anything, one man's confrontation of the deepest and most real implications of such pain.

In certain moments, Charles Bovary reminds us of Prince Myshkin, the "idiot" in Dostoevsky's eponymous novel. It was no accident that Sartre gave his gigantic book on Flaubert, *The Family Idiot*, a similar title. Sartre, however, was referring not to Charles Bovary but to Flaubert himself, to the times when, as a boy, Flaubert separated himself from others with no apparent reason, when he was incapable of uttering a word, when he fell prey to devastating melancholy, to the point of suffering explosive epileptic seizures (Dostoevsky too was an epileptic). For these reasons, he was called "idiot." Flaubert eventually learned how to utilize that identity—so well, in fact, that he was able to transform it into material for his own writing in *L'Idiot des Salons*.

I dreamed that I was in a big forest full of monkeys and my mother was walking with me. The deeper into it we walked, the more of them we saw: they were on the branches laughing and leaping; many entered upon our path, and they got ever larger and more numerous. They stared at me and I began to be afraid. They crowded around and encircled us. One then wanted to caress me and took my hand. I raised my rifle and shot it in the shoulder, making it bleed. It began to shriek horrifically.

My mother then said to me: why do you wound your friend? What did she ever do to you? Don't you see that she loves you? She looks so much like you! And the monkey looked at me. Her gaze tore my soul, and I woke up. (Voyages, *1845*)

Here, in this most vivid prophetic dream, which Flaubert had fully five years before writing *Madame Bovary*, we seem to see an outline of the history of the author's difficult relationship with his character.

The creature on paper becomes the author's "ape": it imitates him, reflects him, pursues him, restores him to himself in a way that frightens him. Flaubert is overwhelmed by disgust, feels threatened. The monkey-character takes his hand and gazes into his eyes. There is nothing aggressive, nothing violent, about the moment: it is only an act, quite accurate, of recognition. But Gustave cannot bear that this creature-character so brazenly forces him to confront himself. So he fires, wounding its shoulder. We should note that Flaubert, like the rest of his friends, described the act of love as "firing a shot" or as "shooting the revolver."

Emma, mortally wounded, shrieks. Gustave's mother at this point asks him why he shoots; his victim is a friend of his, and she even resembles him. From this conversation, we understand that his mother knows what he himself also knows but does not want to acknowledge: the monkey belongs in some deep way to him, is a part of him.

Only the mother and the son know the secret of the mutability and fragility of the monkey; only the mother and the son know how much self-hate and murderous desire the monkey provokes in the author.

"All this is very difficult to explain," Flaubert wrote to Louise, "it has to be felt; you will never feel it, you who are all of one piece, like a beautiful hymn of love and poetry. I am an arabesque in marquetry; there are pieces of ivory, of gold, and of iron; there are some of painted cardboard, some of diamond, and some of tin . . ." (August 21–22, 1846).

The tin and the cardboard call to mind theatrical scenery, a curtain about to open. They remind us of the stage and of a whole world of invention and performance irresistibly attractive to Flaubert's imagination.

If he never became an actor, Flaubert explains to us, that is because he had enough money to loll about a country house and write in peace without having to worry about how to earn a living.

"No doubt I have lived in all those places [France under Louis XIV, ancient Greece and Rome] in some previous existence. I was the manager of a troupe of strolling players under the Roman Empire, I'm certain, one of those queer creatures who went to Sicily to bring women to train as actresses, and were a combination of schoolmaster, pimp and artist. They make an attractive bunch of scoundrels in Plautus's comedies; and when I read them, I seem to have memories. Have you ever felt it, the thrill of antiquity?" (September 4, 1852).

This awareness of a continuous underground theater of the heart and of memory makes Flaubert feel insecure and guilty in his own eyes. But why, we might wonder. What is there about the theater that is so worthy of condemnation?

Here, we run up against the powerful impulse toward wholeness that animates Flaubert's utopian fantasies, product of his religious aspiration to a perfected and identifiable totality. The theater is fragmentation, detachment from the self, caricature and doubleness. It is, therefore, to be condemned.

"Besides, in my state of self-disgust, this isn't the right moment" (August 8, 1851). "I by no means feel the need to write about my memories. My own personality repulses me so much that I feel nauseated. The objects surrounding me seem loathsome or idiotic" (August 24, 1853, to Louis Bouilhet).

Actually, Flaubert did write about his memories—in the beautiful, substantial, and profound letters that he hastily dashed off, often peppered with mistakes, full of self-irony and metaphoric expression.

"I am like those lakes in the Alps that are stirred by the valley breezes (those that blow close to the ground from below); but the strong winds of the mountaintops pass above them without ever wrinkling their surfaces, and only serve to dissipate the fog" (December 28, 1853).

"I was born with all the vices. I radically suppressed some, and underfed the others. . . . My heart is hard, but at least it's solid" (January 13, 1854).

"You ask for love, and complain that I don't send you flowers? . . . Why don't you find some nice budding boy, or a man with fine manners and all the right ideas? I am like the tiger—its member has tufts of stiff hair at the end, which lacerate the female" (February 25, 1854).

"There is something false about my person and my vocation. I was born a lyric poet and I write no verses. I would like to please those that I love, but I make them cry instead" (October 25, 1853).

What falsity was there in his vocation? Such an idea was merely one more brick among the many that made up the house of his self-reproach.

"I laugh at everything, even at that which I most love" (March 27, 1852). But it is a cold, sardonic laugh.

"I was born with many vices, but I never let them come to the surface. I love wine, but I don't drink it; I am a gambler, but I have never touched a card. I like dissoluteness, but I live like a monk. I am a mystic, but I don't believe in anything" (March 8, 1852). He was born, that is to say, with imaginary vices, which were evidently more blameworthy and serious than real ones. Especially if, at times, such vices were enacted inside himself, within the theater of desire.

Emma the monkey is lying in wait. And yet Flaubert wanted to think that if he kept her by his side for three years, it was only in order to "exercise the mind."

"What atrocious work! What a bore! . . . Ah, la *Bovary*! . . . Writing *the mediocre* well, and doing it in such a way that you simultaneously preserve its look, its cut, its very words, this is truly diabolical" (September 12, 1853).

"La Bovary for me was only a question of motive, a theme to develop. Everything I love is not in the book. I will soon send you something more consistent, which takes place in more appropriate settings" (October 30, 1856, to Edma Roger des Genettes).

"I must make enormous efforts to imagine my characters and to make them speak, because they deeply repel me" (August 26, 1853, to Louise).

"This novel of mine indicates much more patience than genius, more work than talent. Not to mention that my style has never been so stiff" (October 5, 1856, to Louis Bouilhet).

"The moral of art consists in its very beauty; more than all other things, I appreciate style first, and then truth. I believe that I have included in my picture some bourgeois manners, and in my exposition of the character of a naturally corrupt woman as much literature and as many familiar traits as was possible, once the topic had been laid out and well established. . . . The commonplace repulses me, and it is precisely because it repulses me that I chose this subject, which is exceedingly common and immutable. This work will have served to limber my fingers; let us move on now to other exercises" (December 12, 1856, to Louis Bonenfant).

Flaubert, that is, distances himself from his character or, rather, from his characters. He has nothing to do with them; he never chose them; he did not want them. It was his friends who insisted; it was the situation; it was a bet, a pretext, a challenge.

"*Madame Bovary* is based on no actual occurrence. It is a *totally fictitious* story; it contains none of my feelings and no details from my own life. . . . It is one of my principles that a writer should not be his own theme. An artist must be in his work like God in creation, invisible and all powerful; he should be everywhere felt, but nowhere seen" (March 18, 1857, to Leroyer de Chantepie).

"Do not judge me by this novel. . . . I am an old angry—or crusty—romantic, whichever you prefer. This book for me was a matter of pure art, of literary intention. Nothing more. . . . It was physically taxing to write. I intend to live (or rather to live again) from now on in a less nauseating environment" (May 5, 1857, to Charles-Augustin Sainte-Beuve).

"And do not compare yourself with la Bovary. You have hardly a thing in common with her. She was not your mental or emotional equal; for she was a slightly perverse character, given to false poetry and false emotion. My first idea was to make her a virgin, living in the depths of the country, growing bitter with age, and so ultimately reaching the depths of religiosity and *imaginary* passion" (March 30, 1857, to Leroyer de Chantepie).

"I have been thick in the head for the last three days. . . . I hope that *Madame Bovary* will have the arsenic in her stomach in a month. Shall I bring her to you when she is buried? I wonder . . ." (September 17, 1855, to Louis Bouilhet).

Is this the ultimate sacrifice made in the melodious name of friendship? Does the violent death of Emma-Louise finally free Flaubert from an enslavement that blocked the path of his relationship with his friends?

But perhaps we will have to wait for *Bouvard and Pécuchet* to finally understand what masculine friendship could mean for Flaubert: the tenderest bond, which, stripped of all sexual desires, literary ambitions, and worldly concerns, in its profound and graceful essence is capable of filling without regret the entire life of a man.

This dream was rendered impossible by the death of his dearest and closest friend, Louis Bouilhet, torn by unexpected illness from an old age they would have shared. But the dream will transform itself into a grand phantasmagoria on paper. And our friend Gustave Flaubert will repair there to take up his abode and to die, far from the menacing monkeys, in a peaceful garden in the French countryside, dreaming of being surrounded by "marble statues and purple draperies, of possessing sofas of hummingbird feathers, carpets of swan skin, armchairs of ebony, parquet of tortoiseshell, chandeliers of gold, and lamps carved of emerald" (January 29, 1854, to Louise Colet).

143

Index